PRAISE FOR
*Blown Away*

"Balanced between compelling story and a brilliant form, *Blown Away* leads us through Boothby's mourning work and, yes, to the wisdom and growth that can come from loss."

—Thomas Brockelman, author
of *Diving for Pearls: Exploring
Philosophy with My Father*

"A soul-piercing account of loss and its miraculous transformation into new life, even creativity. Boothby's autobiography of grappling with his son's addiction and suicide grabs the reader from the first paragraph and gathers force from one page to the next. This book is the most compelling, desperately honest rendering of heartbreak and redemption I have come across: its power is undeniable. It is a gift to anyone who has ever truly suffered."

—Mari Ruti, Distinguished Professor,
University of Toronto

"*Blown Away* is the most aptly titled book I've ever read. No one can read this account of a son's death and the father's aftermath without experiencing it as a life-altering event. Not since Augustine's *Confessions* has a memoir been at the same time a pathbreaking work of philosophy. Boothby takes us from the confrontation with incalculable loss to a meditation on the centrality of absence for living a genuine life. He has converted his despair into a transformative work for everyone who picks it up."

—Todd McGowan, author of *Universality and Identity Politics*

"Immensely moving…Trenchantly and crisply told, this tale will shake your foundations. It did mine."

—C. Edward Robins, STD, PhD, Clinical Director of Dr. Robins & Associates, New York City

"In a narrative as sparklingly insightful as it is excruciatingly heartrending, Richard Boothby tells the riveting story of how he has survived the unsurvivable. Devastated by his son Oliver's addiction-precipitated suicide, this philosopher, one of the world's greatest Lacanian thinkers, was forced by personal tragedy to re-examine not only the intimate details of his life history, but also fundamental ideas about knowledge, love, death, and even God. Like Boothby himself, those who traverse this memoir will gain a hard-won new appreciation of what truly matters in life."

—Adrian Johnston, Distinguished Professor of Philosophy, University of New Mexico

"*Blown Away* is a black mirror into the inner folds of subjectivity and the way haunting traumas try to help the individual to liberate itself from demons that cannot be confronted head-on. The sometimes shocking intimacy of the book makes it a true universal masterpiece."

—Dominik Finkelde, Munich School of Philosophy

"Read in a single sitting that seemed like a single beating of a heart transfixed by this remarkable act of love. One reads this book, as one must, from the deepest register of one's emotional and psychological experience."

—Walter A. Davis, Professor Emeritus, Ohio State University

"In lucid and lyrical prose, Boothby recounts his psychoanalytic exploration of the complex truth that the pain of loss encountered in every tender memory could be the opening to a more profound connection to his son and to himself. It is rare to encounter such a moving and evocative illumination of the essence of a psychoanalytic process."

—Molly Anne Rothenberg, Training and Supervising Analyst, New Orleans-Birmingham Psychoanalytic Center

"The book is well written and makes one feel as if one is reading a Dostoevsky tragedy."

—Wilfried Ver Eecke, author of *Breaking through Schizophrenia: Lacan and Hegel for Talk Therapy*

"*Blown Away* is a remarkable account of grief and recovery—searing, heartfelt, profoundly honest, and dare I say, interesting. The best writing is always, at the core, exploration. This is an epic excavation. What's most satisfying here is the hyper-focus of the lens, the recalibration that cumulatively allows us to come to a new understanding of the experiential world of evolving self-awareness, loss, and finally love."

—Karen Fish, author of *No Chronology*

"It is not easy to write exactingly about the suicide of a loved one, nor the personal revelations that unfold in a rigorous psychoanalysis. Richard Boothby has miraculously managed both, showing us how the tears in the fabric of our being need not be covered over with sentimental fantasies in order to live again, but can become the ground for a new way of knowing what can never be known in any life. I was, to make the difficult pun, blown away by this book."

—Jamieson Webster, author of *Conversion Disorder* and coauthor of *Stay, Illusion!*

*Blown Away*

# *Blown Away*

**REFINDING LIFE
AFTER MY SON'S SUICIDE**

## Richard Boothby

OTHER PRESS
NEW YORK

Aeschylus epigraph translated from the ancient Greek
by Edith Hamilton.

*Production editor: Yvonne E. Cárdenas*
*Text designer: Jennifer Daddio*
*This book was set in Baskerville*
*by Alpha Design & Composition of Pütsfield, NH*

Cover image: Loch Raven Reservoir, Baltimore, Maryland

1 3 5 7 9 10 8 6 4 2

Library of Congress Cataloging-in-Publication Data
Names: Boothby, Richard, 1954- author.
Title: Blown away : refinding life after my son's suicide / Richard Boothby.
Description: New York : Other Press, [2022]
Identifiers: LCCN 2021046077 (print) | LCCN 2021046078 (ebook) |
ISBN 9781635422603 (hardcover) | ISBN 9781635422610 (ebook)
Subjects: LCSH: Suicide. | Sons—Death. | Young adults—Drug use. |
Young adults—Mental health. | Young adults—Suicidal behavior. | Grief.
Classification: LCC HV6546 .B64 2022 (print) | LCC HV6546 (ebook) |
DDC 362.28/3—dc23/eng/20211103
LC record available at https://lccn.loc.gov/2021046077
LC ebook record available at https://lccn.loc.gov/2021046078

*For him.*

*Even in our sleep, pain which cannot forget falls drop by drop*

*upon the heart until, in our own despair, against our will,*

*comes wisdom through the awful grace of God.*

—AESCHYLUS

It's a little oval box. Perched atop the dark, hardwood lid is a little turtle, carved by a skilled hand. Its head is raised, straining from under the shell as if to get a slightly better view.

A gift from me, I found it again when we were going through the things in his apartment. It was the perfect vessel for the scattering. The dark recesses of its rough-grained floor are still lightly dusted with my son's ashes.

# 1

"He's dead!"

The voice on the phone is strained, rasping, almost inhuman. It is a voice frantic with misery, forced to speak yet choked with agony at its own sounding. It's my ex-wife's voice and, to my horror, I know immediately what it is saying.

"He's dead," she says again, her voice lowering to a strangled whisper, the unexpected intimacy of which redoubles its impact. The room spins. I grab for the edge of the table.

I'm outside myself, watching and listening to myself as to some other person, in some other time and place. I see myself look at my watch. Ten minutes to eleven. I feel my mouth begin to move and hear my own voice echoing in some other room. "What's happened, 'Laine? Tell me from the beginning."

*The barest movement of wind brushes her honey-colored hair as the late afternoon sun washes a stand of pines at the far edge of the field, the golden grasses dreamy beneath the green boughs. We are both sixteen, stunned by the amazement of finding a fellow creature to whom we can pour our hearts out.*

"I don't know," she says, and begins to cry. "A policeman came to the door and said I needed to call a number and he gave me a piece of paper with the number written on it. When I saw that it was Anna's number I knew that something terrible had happened."

*He's clowning with my lime-green ski hat pulled down over his two-year-old head, twirling in the middle of the living room floor until he falls down laughing.*

She pauses to gather herself. "The policeman told me he would stay while I called. Anna answered and said, 'He's gone, Elaine.' But I couldn't understand that. 'What do you mean he's gone? Where has he gone?'

"Then Anna said, 'He shot himself, Elaine. He shot himself and he's gone.' And I still couldn't understand that. Had he shot himself and then left? Had he driven off in his truck? Where had he gone? What did that mean, that he's gone? Anna just kept saying that he's gone, he's gone, and I just couldn't understand that."

"Then you know that now for sure? He didn't drive away?'

For a second, I, too, am clinging to an absurd shred of hope that maybe, somehow, he'd only wounded himself and then stumbled out, that maybe by some miracle he'd be okay.

"No, he didn't drive away."

*He turns to look at me from the bow seat of the canoe, his blue eyes grinning under the yellow visor of his Oakland A's cap.*

I take a breath, if only to shake myself clear of that crazy millisecond of hope and brace myself somehow for another wave of the truth.

"So who is with Anna now?" The words are like animals in my mouth.

"The police are there, and her brothers are with her. The ambulance just took him away. Oh, Rick, I can't believe it."

She begins to sob again. "Oh my God, Rick, they took him away! They took my boy away!" Her voice trails off into an anguished wail that cuts into me like a long, jagged blade.

I feel the weight of the pistol in his hand. It's black. Snake smooth. Cold.

"And what about Jackson, is Jack all right?"

She pauses to compose herself again and I can't
help feeling a desperate impatience to know if our
three-and-a-half-year-old grandson is safe.

"Apparently—I don't know how—apparently
he slept through the whole thing. He didn't even
wake up when Emily took him to Anna's parents."

"And where are you?"

There's a long moment of near silence. She is
whimpering, attempting to stifle herself. "I'm at
home," she says. "I need you to come right now."

# 2

All that was fifteen years ago. It can still feel like fifteen minutes.

I had been dreading that phone call. Over months, years, I'd watched my twenty-three-year-old son, Oliver, sink deeper and deeper into drug addiction. An excruciating, slow-motion train wreck.

I had already played his suicide in my mind, anticipated it as a dread possibility, but the event still ripped through me like a giant bomb in the basement. Unbelievably, the walls of the building above still stood, though the internal structure was completely blasted.

In the aftermath, I became obsessed with finding the truth. How had we come to this? What might I have done to prevent it? The need to know was the need to breathe.

I became insatiable, desperate to find the clues from which I could piece together some semblance of an understanding. I pored over his journals and letters. Ransacked drawers stuffed with ticket stubs, bank slips, and photographs. Sifted through his clothes, his shoes, his CDs. Combed through the junk that littered the cab of his pickup truck: the miscellaneous tools, sweatshirts and mismatched gloves, torn and wrinkled maps, spent cigarette packages, boxes of roofing nails, crumpled invoices, empty iced tea cans.

The flip side was a raging intolerance for everything false and superficial. I wanted no silver linings, no sugar-coated platitudes, no phony feel-goodism. I couldn't bear to hear all the expressions of sympathy. Oliver has "passed away." "I'm so sorry for your loss." "He's at peace now." Say it straight, call it *death*. He's *dead*.

Maybe knowing more of the truth was going to hurt, but I wanted to hurt. I wanted to salt my own wound, if only in some crazy way to be with him. I wanted to hold the gun.

I wanted to shoot myself.

It wasn't fear of killing myself that led me to a psychoanalyst, but the burning need to know. To know something about Oliver, and about what led him to kill himself. Also and maybe above all to know something about myself. About my part in the whole catastrophe.

The moment felt all the weirder for the fact that I was no stranger to analysis, though mostly only theoretically. It was reading Freud as an undergraduate that prompted me to set aside the dream of becoming a doctor in favor of a major in philosophy. In those days, study of Freud had already drifted out of medicine and into the humanities. The better part of a half century later—it sometimes seems a bit strange even to me—the intersection between psychoanalytic theory and contemporary philosophy has remained the focus of my career as a college professor. But this was no academic exercise. In the aftermath of Oliver's death, I was bleeding to death myself.

This book is about a father's attempt to stanch the greatest possible wound with some measure of understanding. Putting down the phone that night, my world no longer made sense to me. I had lost the primary thing, the one thing I would unhesitatingly have given my life for. In fact, I felt like I was already dead. Just still walking around.

It was that desperate need for understanding that drove me into the terrible silence of an analyst's consulting room. It was the beginning of a long period of nausea, in which the only thing greater than the pain of talking was the torment of saying nothing. It would be a long period of relentless questioning, very much including obsessively questioning my own questions. My son's death plunged me into a long and anguished period of self-interrogation.

But then, after some years of being crippled by grief, something surprising happened. I seemed again to find myself, and to refind life, almost against my will. This unexpected but deeply revitalizing result was in large part a hard-won fruit of my time in analysis. The painful prerequisite was realizing that I was not the person I had always taken myself to be.

The strangest thing of all is that what finally gave me some feeling of peace and a renewed sense of life was coming to accept what I didn't know, what I could not know. It was an outcome I would never have predicted, a result especially unlikely for a philosophy professor, someone for whom the pursuit of knowledge and understanding has been a lifelong passion. In fact, it was a shift that pretty much took the knees out from under my whole philosophical outlook. It was a step away from the satisfactions of theoretical clarity toward tolerating, even embracing, my own uncertainties. And yet I can only think that it was an improvement. Making some peace with my own void of unknowing left me with a new feeling of calm and a completely unanticipated sense of richness and rebirth.

This book is an attempt to tell that strange story.

# 3

Hanging up the phone, I glance across the room at Rebecca. Her eyes are wide with alarm. "He's killed himself," I blurt out, choking back tears, shocked at what I myself am saying. "Oliver shot himself."

Her breath catches and her hand claps over her mouth in an involuntary reflex of horror.

The thought absurdly flashes into my mind, as though I'm lecturing to one of my classes: "This is the very face of panic, the quintessential expression of stunned terror. It's the standard face on posters for B-rated horror movies." A gaggle of such faces flit into view—Joan Fontaine or Tippi Hedren in cringing, wild-eyed grimaces. This must be a movie. You've seen this before.

"I have to go," I say, breaking a silence of seconds that feels like eons.

"I know," Rebecca says, squeezing me tightly to her, "I know, I know, I'm so sorry. Oh God, Rick, I'm so sorry." The look on her face is one of infinite sympathy. She knew that this outcome was a possibility. We had worried and talked about it for months.

"Don't think about me. I know you have to go."

Her arms are around me, and I'm overcome with wordless gratitude. Only later did it occur to me to think about how awkward and confusing it must have been for her, barely a year into our marriage, to give me over to my ex-wife in the middle of the night. And how hard it must have been for her to stay behind, as yet unaware of any of the details of what had happened, unable to contribute anything helpful beyond resisting her own urge to ask questions, unsure when she would see me again. Unsure of everything.

———

Charged with the force of emergency, I run every red light on the way. *He's dead.* The phrase keeps repeating in my head but refuses to register as real.

I fully expect to play the role of the comforter when I arrive. It's like a mission I've assigned to myself. Even when Elaine appears at the threshold and looks up at me, her eyes red and watery, her face pale and quivering, her hair disheveled, I feel fairly steady. But as she throws herself on me, her body convulsed with little cries, I myself break down and burst into uncontrollable weeping. I am crushed by my own sobs.

"I need to sit down," I say at last, and make my way to her living room.

Settling on the couch, I think perhaps the worst is over, but looking up at her again, her eyes on mine with childlike pain and fear, as if imploring me to do something, to tell her that she needn't worry, to somehow make it all better, I again completely dissolve into sobbing. I am washed over by the unbearable realization that there is nothing I can do. The worst possible thing has happened, the event from which there can be no recovery, the outcome that makes every further effort useless. I am suffocating. Struggling to regain myself, even to breathe. The growing darkness only deepens.

My shaking finally begins to ease. A strange relaxation settles over me, like the otherworldly stillness after a violent summer squall. I pick up her pack of Marlboro Lights. I haven't smoked a cigarette in years. I light one and greedily, gratefully inhale. From the very first drag, I am acutely aware of the sense of connection it affords with him. He had an odd, extra-intense way of smoking—pulling a second time on his cigarette while a portion of the first puff would begin curling from his nostrils. Automatically and without thinking, I find myself doing the same thing.

"Do you have anything to drink?"

She has a bottle of vodka, which I take straight, she with tonic water. And thus we sit for another hour or more, smoking and drinking. The overall effect—produced by the nicotine and alcohol, to be sure, by the gratification of having something to occupy our hands, but above all by the reassurance of simply sitting together in a quiet solidarity of pain—is deeply calming for both of us. She retells the story of the policeman's arrival at the house about ten-thirty at night, his enigmatic insistence that she call a phone number she recognized to be Anna's, and her confusion over Anna's saying, "He's gone."

I repeatedly press her for more details, only some of which she knows. We consider calling Anna but reject the idea. Her brothers and sister had come not long after the police arrived. After the body was taken and the police left, she had gone to her brother's for the night. Her sister Emily had scooped up little Jack from his bed and trundled him off to her parents' house. Eventually we both fall into a long silence. It is agonizingly clear that there is nothing to be done. Nothing even to say.

"I have to go to bed," she weakly says at last. She's obviously exhausted. "But can you please stay with me?"

"I'll sleep right here on the couch."

"No. Please, I need you to sleep beside me."

"Of course," I say without hestitation, oblivious for the moment to the strangeness of crawling into bed with my divorced wife, though I tell her that she might go on ahead of me. I need to stay up a while longer, if only because for me falling asleep will require a good deal more vodka. For her part, Elaine is completely drained.

My arrival allowed something in her to release,
as if she had been physically clinging to Oliver
and now, relieved temporarily by my presence,
she can let go for a moment and rest. After calling
Becky to let her know that I won't be coming
home, I find myself alone in the darkness.

*A random series of memories flicker before my mind. An
eager, wide-eyed four-year-old, he's running toward me along
the foamy strand at Crane's Beach. I push him on a swing
in the park at Fresh Pond. I am reading him* The Lorax,
*his bony form curled up tightly beneath my arm. He knows
the words by heart and immediately chides me if I skip a
page. We're cooking pancakes in the Somerville apartment
on a Sunday morning. He's standing on the kitchen chair,
a metal spatula gripped tight in his hand, smiling up at
me. My voice is already hoarse from ventriloquizing the
exaggerated whisper of his invisible friend, Stanley.*

*Suddenly the lights of a police car throb. The back of
my neck tingles with a dreadful electricity. I see his lifeless
body trundled into an ambulance. I see the sheets soaked
with blood.*

Elaine is asleep when I come into the bedroom.
Curled up on her side, she looks impossibly small.
As I crawl into the bed she stirs. I know this feeling

with perfect intimacy, born of our twenty-two years of marriage. Yet that marriage ended some six years ago, and now, feeling the warmth of her body just inches away from me, hearing her breathing, I'm overcome by a terrible wave of regret and despair. The breakup of our marriage left me injured and exhausted in a way that made me wonder if I would ever recover. Now, my lungs wheezy from two hours of continuous smoking and my head clouded with drink, the entirety of the past, already broken by our divorce, seems sucked into the grave.

I wake up alone. It takes me a moment to realize where I am and a few seconds longer to remember why I am there. It might be any other morning, save finding myself inexplicably in my ex-wife's bed. Then it washes over me with nauseating force: the horrendous news that Oliver has shot himself, the wave of panic, the desperate need to do something, anything, then the sickening realization of my helplessness, the collapse into impotent despair.

Elaine sits at the kitchen table staring blankly out the window into the tranquil yard in back of her apartment. She stands up as I enter and, as we silently embrace, she again begins to cry. For a long time neither of us is able to say anything. We simply stand there as if the physical mass of the other is the only stable thing left in the world. At last she breaks away from me, suddenly charged with some rogue energy. "But where is he, Rick? Where did they take him? I have to know where he is."

The answer to this question—the thought had already passed through my mind last night—seems obvious to me. His body would have been taken by the police to a morgue. My mind had already been visited by images of stainless steel gurneys and those horrible body drawers.

"But you said last night that he had been taken away by ambulance," I begin.

"We should have been there," she says. "He was all alone. We should have been there."

Her insistence brings me up short with the force of an accusation. It had not even occurred to me to go to him. Why not? Wasn't there something shameful in that? Shouldn't I have rushed to his side no matter what?

———

We spend much of the morning as we had those hours of the night, sitting together on the couch smoking, alternating between fits of crying and periods of stunned silence. The phone calls to relatives only renew the spasms of pain. Oliver dies that day over and over again.

Elaine's sister Ann arranges to be on the Southwest flight to Baltimore that afternoon. When we return from picking her up at the airport, we again settle into the living room, bruised and brooding, grateful for a new pack of cigarettes and for the way Ann's arrival and shared tears buoy us up. Momentarily distracted, I notice several familiar pieces of furniture—the old wicker couch, the walnut drop-leaf table, and the prim little Windsor chair my mother painted lime green. They are the leftovers from the sale of the old cottage at Turner, my family's summer place in Maine, only an hour from our house in Cumberland but a world away.

A short time later, Elaine's friend Michelle arrives. With the little apartment starting to fill up with people, I begin to feel a welcome sense of numbed distance from the rawness and violence of the first encounter with Oliver's death. We resignedly agree that he would have wished to be cremated and Michelle calls a funeral home she knows about. Neither Elaine nor I can muster the energy or focus to deal with such things. I stay on for another hour or so, but I also need to get away. I'm seduced by the idea that it will be easier for me once I'm home with Rebecca. She must be worried.

We met six years ago, only four or five months after my separation from Elaine. I had watched her for years in the violin section of the Baltimore Symphony and, finding myself alone at a Sunday afternoon concert, I was suddenly fired up by a crazy, half-thought impulse. Why not meet her? I took up a position just outside the stage door, hoping to catch her coming out.

I told myself it was just curiosity, merely a matter of wanting to know why this woman had so long turned my eye. She's almost certainly married, anyway, I thought, or has a boyfriend. But when I caught up with her on the street and felt instantly enchanted by her, I comically realized I had made something of a problem for myself. I hardly felt ready for getting so quickly into a new relationship.

It was almost four years before we moved in together—I wanted and needed to go slow—but it was a magical four years. Despite our very different professional lives, an artist and an academic, something clicked between us in a way that neither of us had ever felt before.

Rebecca had a ten-year-old son from a previous marriage, a circumstance that created a welcome symmetry between us, one all the more reassuring for the fact that her son, Dewey, had difficulties of his own—Asperger's syndrome (as they called it then), complicated by a cleft palate and a substantial hearing impairment. It shames me to admit it, but Dewey's challenges made it a little easier on me that my own son seemed increasingly consumed by problems.

Arriving at home, for a while things seem stable enough. Though I still have little appetite, sitting for dinner with Bec and Dewey is a deeply welcome respite. It takes the better part of an hour to fill her in on what has happened, the details of which I rehearse with a certain degree of clinical detachment. She is no stranger to death, having been particularly affected by the recent death of her ex-husband, with whom she had remained close after their divorce, mostly as a consequence of their mutual responsibility for Dewey. Not so very different from my enduring closeness to Elaine. Once again I'm overwhelmed with gratitude for her support.

But settling by myself at the desk in my study after dinner I become completely unglued. The waves of sobbing are relentless. Choking with the convulsions of grief, I think that I myself will die from the sheer force of suffocating, stomach-twisting tears.

How did we get to this place of such complete desolation? It's the helplessness wrought by the irreversibility of events, the unspeakable agony of something done that can never be undone.

His finger is on the trigger. Do I keep returning to it because I imagine that the inner secret of Oliver's death, perhaps even the secret of his life, might be somehow contained in that instant, sealed and frozen forever like an insect in amber? Would that secret be revealed to me if only I could know what was in his mind in that final moment?

His finger presses. At what point will it release the firing mechanism? At what point will it change everything? At what point will he be blasted out of existence?

Perhaps he even flirted with that very uncertainty. Perhaps he played distractedly with that expertise in firearms that gave him such dark pleasure during the last two or three years of his life. Was it, at that last moment, a desperate, heart-aching game of chicken?

Or maybe in the distraction that only the deepest despair can spawn, his mind was more or less a blank. Did he really mean to pull the trigger? What if the trigger had released but the gun miraculously jammed and failed to discharge? What if he had heard the crisp click of its inner mechanism, startlingly loud, but nothing compared with the deafening report of the bullet's firing? Had that happened, might he have recoiled in terror and loathing—"Oh my God, I almost shot myself! What an idiot I am! Thank God the damned thing didn't go off!"? And so he might have jumped back from the brink of death, horrified by his own recklessness, perhaps even bolstered by a renewed sense of the value of life.

*But it did go off.* And if his death was no real choice but rather an unintended blink of chance, how could I bear it? Wouldn't it be all the more excruciating for being an absurd, arbitrary accident?

But then again, maybe none of that is right. Maybe he sat there on the bed, a welter of thoughts spinning through his mind, desperate to find some way out of the predicament in which he now found himself, all the while despising himself for his own failures and sinking into an ever-darker, ever-shrinking vortex. Maybe all he wanted was to thrust the whole mess away from himself, as one might spit out a plum pit or flick away the butt of an exhausted cigarette.

# 4

I'm looking at a photograph of the two of us in Colorado. It's strange, I have no idea who took it.

*And then I'm with him.*

*It's already early in the afternoon and we've just left the city limits of Denver, driving south. A father-son trip was Elaine's idea, a kind of reward for Oliver's completion of a rocky first year of high school.*

*It's Oliver's idea, four hours into our journey south, to simply pull over and step into the yawning vastness of the Colorado desert, an open sea of delicate grasses and sagebrush extending for miles in every direction. To the west, the mountains are already shadowed by the slanting sun of the late afternoon. We stand in the silence, momentarily paralyzed by the sheer enormity and utter stillness. There's no other car in sight. The air hangs unmoving in the glinting sun. The buzzing of a passing insect seems impossibly loud.*

*Great Sand Dunes National Monument is a fitting destination. For reasons neither of us know, maybe an odd wrinkle of the genetic code, we're both strangely drawn to desert landscapes. Is it their serene expansiveness? The challenge of an inhospitable environment? The perverse appeal of lonely places?*

*We arrive toward the very end of the day, the searing midday heat now past and the landscape bathed in the golden light of the sinking sun. The sight of the dunes looming a mile or two distant is too much for either of us to resist and, tired though we are from the flight from Baltimore in the morning and the drive south from Denver during the afternoon, we set off for a hike into the sand hills.*

*Lying just west of the Sangre de Christo Mountains, the Great Sand Dunes comprise some sixty square miles of almost perfectly unbroken sand, rising in peaks up to eight hundred feet high. Its unusual topography is formed, the ranger at the campground told us, by sand dropped by the wind as it sweeps across the long, flat stretch of desert* to the west and swirls at the foot of the mountain wall at the desert's eastern edge. As we leave the parking lot, we cross a broad, dry streambed, then head off into the great waves of sand. The sidelight of evening only enhances the dramatic crests and delicate ripples of the wind-sculpted landscape. Its sublime beauty compensates us for the difficulty of trudging a mile or more out into the dunes, which we now have all to ourselves.

With the setting of the sun, we are treated to a ceiling of stars whose brilliance steadily intensifies with the gathering darkness until it seems that they wink at our fingertips. Meanwhile, a fresh night wind has come up, from which we take refuge in a deep valley between towering peaks of sand. Into this cleft the wind cannot penetrate and we break out the camp stove and cook two heaping bowls of instant macaroni and cheese, one of those humble hiking meals that seem impossibly delicious. We lie back on the sand, already surprisingly cool and moist against our T-shirts, and gaze at the canopy of stars overhead. We talk in hushed tones, as if inhibited by the magnificence of the place, like tourists silenced by the interior of a great cathedral.

"We did the right thing, Dad."

"You mean coming to Colorado?"

"Yeah, but also coming out here tonight. This place is awesome."

"You're right, it's incredible. I've never seen dunes like these. They remind me of The Crab with the Golden Claws, when Tintin and Captain Haddock are in the middle of the Sahara."

"Yeah, and you're Captain Haddock!" Oliver says laughing.

"What do you mean?" I say, only half-kidding, "I always thought of myself as Tintin."

"No way, Dad!" he says. "Captain Haddock's the sailor man. The drunken sailor. That's you."

"Well, that makes you Tintin, Oliver. Do you think that's right?"

He seems to reflect for a moment, maybe flipping through the stack of Tintin chronicles we read together over the years of his childhood.

"Yeah, I'm Tintin," he says. "Tintin's always looking for something."

"Right, the boy detective. So what are you looking for?"

He pauses and grins up at me in the starlight. "I guess I'll only know when I find it."

It's almost midnight when we rouse ourselves for the trek back to the car, but upon climbing to the rim of our valley refuge, it's clear that we have no sure idea where we are. I know the stars well enough to get a rough sense of the easterly direction of the park entrance, but the wind-blown

34

sand has long ago erased our tracks and the precise heading for our retreat from the dunes is impossible to reckon. No matter. If we go far enough east we'll hit the streambed we crossed just after leaving the parking lot and from there we can find our way to the road. I extol the adventure appeal of this plan, but I also can't suppress a growing anxiety. We have no extra clothes beyond the T-shirts and shorts in which we endured the midday heat and we're both beginning to shiver with cold.

Our plan only half works. We succeed in finding the streambed, but in the three or four hours we've been gone, things have ominously changed. Bone dry when we traversed it in the early evening, the channel has become a rush of water, deep and swift-moving enough to give us serious pause in crossing it. I distract myself from my renewed anxiety by speculating upon possible causes of this unexpected development. Could this torrent of water be the result of the night air's altered rate of evaporation? Is it possible that the contents of this roiling sluiceway, now an imposing obstacle to our getting back to the car, would in the heat of the day have passed off invisibly into the desert air?

"Dad," says Oliver, "you've got to be kidding. Your philosopher brain is overheating again. It's probably just irrigation water. It's getting released upstream someplace to water some farmers' fields down the valley."

Despite feeling mildly snubbed by this retort, I have to admit that his is the far more likely explanation. Though I remain secretly attracted to my own theory, preposterous as it probably is, I feel proud of him for coming up with a clearly better one.

The daunting prospect of fording the stream is made even more intimidating by a steep embankment on the opposite shore, densely overgrown with brush. Better, we think, to skirt downstream in hopes of finding a more inviting landing. Hurried by the night chill and by the desire to reach the car and our waiting bedrolls, we walk along the edge of the stream until the unfamiliar topography makes it increasingly clear that we have misjudged our bearings and hiked in the wrong direction. The trail to the parking lot lies upstream, not down. Turning around with a groan, we again set off, now laboring as much to keep our spirits up as to keep our feet moving.

As another half hour passes, the quantity of water in the stream seems only to have increased. It's now or never. We strip off our shoes and wade cautiously into the flood, our feet sinking deep into the soft sand of the streambed, the frigid water soaking the hems of our shorts. The force of the current continually sets us off balance and I'm afraid that one or both of us will keel over in the rapid.

We succeed in reaching the opposite shore but then face the barrier of the embankment, with the great tangle of dense bushes at its upper edge. Though the sand maddeningly gives way with each attempt to mount higher and the crowning thicket poses a final, demonic impediment, we finally break out, scratched and breathless, on a table of pancake-flat desert dotted with cacti and sagebrush. Somewhere beyond this plain lies the road that will lead us to the car. But crossing it turns out to be another unexpected challenge. Just a hundred yards into the trek, Oliver, improbably clad in Birkenstock sandals over woolen socks, begins to suffer mightily from the pricking spines of low-lying cacti, impossible to avoid in the darkness.

To this point, I hadn't really noticed Oliver's footgear and I'm momentarily annoyed at his impractical choice. We press on for a while until his yelping forces a radical decision. I'll have to carry him. Yet no sooner have I saddled him on my back than an especially repulsive thought occurs to me: the nighttime desert landscape in which we find ourselves might well be acrawl with rattlesnakes. Whatever shred of rational fear there might be in this thought joins forces with my childhood phobia of snakes. The path ahead is transformed into a minefield of reptilian horrors.

As I struggle to master myself in the face of this new challenge, my neurotic dread, as if mocking me with its capacity to keep the upper hand, succeeds in drawing my *more rational side in common cause. If by some crazy twist of bad luck I get bitten, surely Oliver can't carry me, shoes or no shoes, and there we'll be, a mile from the road in the darkness of the Colorado night with a venomous snake bite. There's only one solution. We've got to return to the thicket of bushes at the stream's edge and cast about for a stick with which to warn the local serpents of our approach. Another half hour later, having found a plausible stick, we again set out for the road.*

*I puff and grunt with Oliver on my back while he pokes ahead of us as best he can with the stick. It's a ludicrous spectacle and more than once in the long march to the road we both choke with laughter. A three-hundred-pound, four-armed man poking his way across the Colorado desert in the middle of the night.*

# 5

I lie back awkwardly and try to relax, painfully
aware of the woman sitting unseen behind me.
The flow of time seems bizarrely disturbed,
moving both faster and slower than it should.
Every impulse to speak catches in my throat like
a fish bone.

Dr. Barbara Frankel. Like a lot of psychoanalysts,
her consulting room is in her home, a boxy, flat-
roofed addition in the back. It's a big old place—a
gray, wood frame house surrounded by tall trees.

The day I arrive to start my analysis is not my first visit. I started seeing her less than a month after Oliver's death. Once a week, "face-to-face," as they say in the trade. But it quickly became clear that I needed the more intensive version. Four times a week on the couch.

I had briefly been in analysis before. Three years earlier, I had spent a spring-term sabbatical in Paris. The primary task was to finish the last couple of chapters for a book about the work of the French psychoanalyst Jacques Lacan. The sideline was to enter a short-term analysis with one of Lacan's followers, Moustafa Safouan, an elderly Egyptian émigré with a magically quiet and gentle manner. It was to be what the French charmingly call *une tranche d'analyse*, "a slice of analysis," as if it were a dessert course. But four months into my planned half year with Safouan, I had to rush back home when I got the call. Oliver had attempted to kill himself.

It was, a psychiatrist later told us, the sort of quasi-theatrical act intended less to really do himself in than to register a cry for help. At the end of the afternoon, right around the time when

he knew that Elaine would be coming home
from work, he climbed into the bathtub and cut
himself—across the wrist rather than the much
more deadly cut parallel with the arteries.

I settle my head against the leaf of paper that shields
the pillow on Barbara's couch. Damp with an
anxious sweat, I look around the room as if for the
first time. Three walls are generously apportioned
with windows open upon the lush foliage of trees in
back of the house. The fourth is lined with books. I
am momentarily distracted from my discomfort by
the gentle tapping on the roof.

The rain reminds me of the rain on the roof of
the old cottage in Turner.

I'm obeying the basic rule of psychoanalysis:
to say whatever comes into your head, however
apparently trivial or irrelevant, even nonsensical.
But at least for now, it isn't hard for me. The
words come by themselves.

That much I had already learned from my time
with Safouan. Just let the words tumble out,
allowing the speech stream to flow unimpeded

by self-consciousness. In the very few times that Safouan himself spoke, it was usually simply to repeat one or more of my words. The effect was almost always shocking, like the addition of a punctuation mark that changes the whole meaning of a sentence.

The effects of his silences were equally powerful, at times even more so. At the end of my admitting something shameful or having just related a particularly painful memory, his silence could stun me, as if I'd been struck with a blunt object. In that silence my own words would come back to me as if someone else had uttered them. It's the most basic tenet of Lacan's teaching. Regardless of our intentions, we almost always say something more than we mean to.

At least, I continue, it was what anyone else would have called a "cottage." My grandparents—it now seems a bit strange to me—my grandparents always used to call it "the Camp."

It was a ramshackle ark of a place, roughly built with high ceilings, walls of knotty pine, and big porches on all four sides. It was—like this house—painted battleship gray. My grandfather bought it for a thousand dollars in the early 1930s. For another five hundred he got nearly as many acres of woodland on the north end of the lake. Pleasant Pond in Turner, Maine. An out-of-the-way place in a distinctly out-of-the-way state. It was the scene of my most indelible childhood memories. I still dream about it.

But why am I telling her all this? What's the point?

What's the point of anything now?

In the helpless pause that follows, I already regret getting back into analysis at all. It almost feels like something I owe him. The least I can do after everything that's happened. But it also feels self-indulgent.

As if taking refuge in an absurd distraction, I'm suddenly struck by the pleasant smell of Barbara's consulting room—soap and coffee floating agreeably above the tarry odor of a cold fireplace. That same smell would come to me as I lay balled up under the covers in the early mornings at Turner, when the cottage was still dark and the fire in the back kitchen woodstove had long since gone out. I'd hear the stove lids clank and catch the first sweet whiff of burning newspaper. As usual, my grandfather was up before anyone else, lighting a fire. It wouldn't be long before a draft of warmer air would course up the narrow back stairs.

Oliver and I went there often when he was little. Not to the old cottage—my parents were forced to sell the place some years before he was born—but to the shoreline expanse of woods at the north end of the lake. It was the grove of tall pines that my grandmother called the Picnic Grounds. During the years I was in graduate school, I became obsessed with cutting a road through the woods to the water's edge and clearing the tangle of dead trees and brush to open a spot for camping.

He was four years old the first time we went there by ourselves, three hours' drive from Boston. No fan of tent camping, to say nothing of the mosquitoes, Elaine often skipped our trips to Turner, but Oliver loved them. His favorite times were when we'd burn the great heaps of cut branches and blowdown. We'd douse the pile with gasoline and touch it off, an instant mushrooming inferno, and we'd dance around with wild abandon, the trees above our heads like a cathedral. The fires were especially magical after nightfall. Every time you'd throw on a log, a cloud of orange sparks would gyre up into the darkness.

And turtle hunting. Oliver loved turtle hunting. I got good at catching them when I was a kid, mostly the yellow-bottomed "painted" turtles, their sides flecked with red, though also every once in a while one of the giant snappers that terrified my little sister. At the Picnic Grounds, the best time was on sunny mornings, when the painted turtles would climb out to bask on logs along the shore. I'd paddle a few last, deep strokes and let the canoe glide silently toward them and Oliver would make a swipe from the bow with the net just as they plopped into the water. Many a morning we'd catch half a dozen. We'd leave them pawing around in the bottom of the boat until our midday swim and then let them go, watching them paddle furiously for the deep water.

*"Come on, Dad, I think I see one." He's pulling at my sleeping bag. I groan, stiff and bleary-eyed. "Come on, come on," he says, "I've got the net. We're ready to go!" It's barely dawn and he's already been out scouting the prospects along the shoreline.*

It's unbearable, I say, interrupting myself.

"Unbearable?" Barbara asks in the pause.

I can't help thinking about the days at Turner, but with Oliver dead, it's excruciating. The times we had together were such exquisite pleasure. It makes what I feel now all the more awful.

Barbara says nothing.

Why am I paying a hundred bucks an hour to rehearse these old memories? Because Turner was so important to him? He'd named Jack after it—"Jackson Turner Boothby"—a measure of the depth and fondness of Oliver's memories of the place.

But now the question strangely presses on me—I never before thought to wonder about it—what did the Turner connection really mean to him? The times Oliver and I spent there were incredibly precious to me, but what was it for him?

Another long pause. I'm too caught up in my own thoughts to say anything.

"You don't know what it really meant to him," Barbara says, as if bringing me back to the topic.

No. I don't know. We did the usual father-son stuff—camping, making fires, chopping with a hatchet, roasting hot dogs on a stick—and there was the boat and our turtles. Golden memories. But I think there was something else. It was as if something was being transmitted between us. I suppose it was something I had taken from Turner as a child that I very much wanted to pass on to him.

"So maybe it's also a matter of what Turner really meant to you?" she says.

The question rings in my ears and suddenly makes it seem odd that I seized first on the memories of the fires and the turtles. Why those memories?

At least part of the answer seems clear, in fact I'd made the connection already. The bonfires and turtles were the links, like quilting points, between the Turner of my youth and the one I tried to re-create with Oliver. The sale of the cottage cut him off from the throng of other memories of my own summers there, memories that now rush back.

The old place had us constantly working. We jokingly called it "Achin' Acres." We were always cutting down trees and hauling the limbs away— we had many a great bonfire in those days. I remember the year we scraped and painted the porch floors that ran around all four sides of the house. There was the summer we replaced the rotted stretch of cedar fence along the road. Or when we built the diving float, pouring a huge wooden box full of concrete for an anchor. We dragged it down the beach and into the water on wooden rollers—"the Pharaoh method," my father called it.

My grandfather was my father's constant partner on every work detail...

"Your father's father?"

Yes, the one for whom I'm named. Richard
Perkins Boothby. My father's Junior and I'm the
Third. We called him "Worker Perk." He had a
trunk of special Turner clothes out in the garage
that we kidded him about. One summer my
brother painted a sign on it: "Gramp's Costumes
and Disguises." My grandfather was a small, thin
man who enjoyed style and wore clothes well,
but at Turner he'd have baggy overalls, dabbed
with paint and smelling of turpentine, flannel
shirts holed at the elbows, hobnail boots from
the war—the first, not the second—or canvas
sneakers the likes of which nobody'd ever seen.
And hats. He'd always have on some hopeless,
rumpled thing. My grandmother was always
complaining about them.

There was a perfect intimacy between my
grandfather and my father. "Worker Perk" fit
my father, too. I was awed by the record of their
bigger projects, impressively inscribed on the door
frame of the garage. "Garage moved North of
house, 1938." "Living room fireplace built, 1947."

"Windmill and tank replaced with electric pump, 1956." "Back bedrooms finished, 1962."

"Maybe you hoped that you and Oliver might be as close as your father had been with his father."

I ignore her comment, as if recalling the memories of my own childhood at the cottage has induced a sort of trance in which I am happy to lose myself.

I was fascinated by the old garage. It was less a garage than a workshop and storehouse. It had two great side-by-side doors that swung wide. Inside was an incredible congeries of tools and gear, stuff that would have been familiar to a Maine farmer a century ago, but that struck a suburban kid like me as wondrously exotic. A pair of wooden wagon wheels hung from the rafters. In one corner there was a galvanized, two-handled milk can as tall as my sister. On one wall hung a two-handled bucksaw, six feet long, and two huge, snakelike scythes. Farther along were several big metal washtubs, three feet in diameter. Above the workbench, with its massive vise, the wall was lined with dozens of bottles of nails, screws, hooks, hasps, and hinges. Beneath were lengths of heavy chain and coils of tarred rope, fitted with block and tackle. To the side was a huge wooden tool chest hinged with extra-heavy hardware, stenciled with lettering that said PROPERTY OF U.S. ARMY.

I loved the garage, but more as a wonderland than a workshop. My one-year-older brother Jim was the real worker. In fact, he was a demon for work. He'd do anything to please my father and grandfather. His willingness to work became a mini-legend in the family. I sometimes hated him for it. In school and sports, too, he was a dogged striver. I was the dreamer, not so much lazy as just distracted. For me, the real magic of Turner was in the woods and out on the lake. Slipping off by myself into the silence beneath the pines, wandering along the beach to catch frogs and newts, or simply perching myself on the rocks at the south end of the cove to follow the dance of a school of golden shiners—those were my favorite occupations.

I loved the baked bean dinners on Saturday nights, especially when we'd eat out on the big porch. My grandmother put the stiff, white beans on to cook in the early morning. By late afternoon, they'd be the color of good shoe leather and the house would be filled with the heady fragrance of salt pork and molasses.

On rainy nights we'd eat in the living room, with its enormous stone fireplace. The floor was covered by a pair of unusual rugs, woven hemp in complicated geometrics of brown and white. The story was that the previous owner, Clement Lampson, compelled by a painful divorce to sell the house with everything in it, brought those rugs from India. Also in the living room was an old-fashioned player piano. It had only one roll of music. The tune was always "Three O'Clock in the Morning."

I even loved burning the trash. During our stays at the cottage we burned what we could in an open, stone fireplace away from the house. I'd build trash cities from the paper towel rolls, milk cartons, and pasta boxes and then set them ablaze. Bigger stuff that couldn't be burned we took to the town dump at Snake Pond.

It's unbelievable, isn't it?

Am I trying to reenlist Barbara in my reveries?
Checking to make sure she's still listening?

"Unbelievable?"

Unbelievable that I'm not making up the name—
almost too perfect for a dump. Snake Pond was
in fact a small lake, at one time probably a lovely
Maine spot, set in a deep depression surrounded
by woods. There was no caretaker overseeing the
place, just a narrow dirt road that split the lake
in two, itself formed by countless years of trash
dumping.

Why am I recounting this stream of memories?
I don't know. I'm savoring them now, but it seems
ridiculous to be paying such an exorbitant amount
for the hearing of them.

Then it occurs to me, like a cold hand on the
neck. The digression about the pond dump
allowed me to avoid talking about the painful
fate of the piano.

One year, for reasons that escape me now, or
perhaps I never knew, the decision was made

to get rid of the old piano. But what to do with it? "Take it to Snake Pond," said my father, as if that were the only possible course of action. Whereupon my older brother convinced him to let us smash it to pieces before carting the wreckage off to the dump.

I still can't believe that my father allowed it. My brother and I somehow managed to get the piano out of the house—no doubt more of the Pharoah method—and there it sat, weirdly out of place in the shade of the pine trees. I'll never forget my brother, his eyes wide with the giddy thrill of it, swinging the first blow of the sledgehammer. It ripped into the neat line of keys and buckled their supportive wooden shelf. The thing reverberated with an absurdly complex, twanging chord. Even at the time, the whole episode felt vaguely criminal, a needless waste. To think of it now, even after all these years, makes me feel sick.

Turner has always floated in my memory as the touchstone of my childhood happiness, as a sort of golden place in which not even a long rainy day could dampen my spirits. But now a doubt inserts itself. Was it quite so seamlessly happy? Hearing my own stories of Turner through Barbara's ears makes me hear them differently, bringing out the minor key. Or is it just that recalling those stories now, caught up in the agony of Oliver's death, the whole bank of memories, even the happiest of them, can only be renewed occasions for pain? All the more painful for having once been happy.

The image of the smashed piano then returns in dreadful tandem with that of Oliver's mortally wounded body, and with it, a desperate and choking realization that the sound of his voice, like the plink of that old piano, is gone forever. I will never again hear that voice. Never again feel his chest press against me in a hug hello, or even a hug goodbye.

My long-winded account of Turner—it now seems painfully obvious—was a means of staving off this wretched sadness. Did I think that I could somehow escape the agony of the present by taking refuge in the past?

Barbara finally breaks the silence of my tears. "That's all the time we have for today."

# 6

Awakening on Tuesday morning, dulled
from having again drunk myself to sleep, I'm
once more spared any awareness of what has
happened. I roll over onto my back and draw in
a deep breath. But as the elements of the world
reassemble themselves, it hits me like a blow to
the head. My son has shot himself to death. For
several minutes I lie helpless, as if strapped to
the bed like a torture victim while the horrible
particulars reload in my consciousness.

My thoughts turn quickly to Elaine. I'm already seeking a way out of my own panic and agony by playing the rescuer. Then I remember that her sister Ann is with her. I can relax a little. At least she isn't alone.

Rebecca lies silently beside me. After his first suicide attempt, four years after my breakup with Elaine and three years before the one that killed him, Oliver moved in with Becky, Dewey, and me, and we lived together as a foursome for a year. It was a tough period in many ways, but Oliver seemed to get his feet back under him. In October he landed a job as an apprentice with Fick Bros., the roofing outfit, and the following June, seeming a good deal more stable, he moved out into an apartment of his own. A year after that, Bec and I got married.

She is awake but says nothing. When I turn to look at her, she meets my eyes with a gaze that seems to acknowledge every increment of the excruciating gauntlet I'm going through. It is only then, seeing her look back at me, that I break down in tears. She wriggles up to me, but I find it almost impossible to respond.

Is everything in my existence from now on going to be like this? I am incredibly grateful for her embrace yet can't accept it. She graciously forgives this crippled reaction, strokes my head and says gently, "I understand."

How can she understand? I certainly don't. In a situation like this, what does it even mean for someone to say "I understand"? What is to be understood about the terrible finality of death? Only, I suppose, that its effect on us is unspeakable pain. Death condemns us to an unbearable, unthinkable emptiness.

Elaine calls not long after. Oliver's body has been transferred from the morgue to the funeral home. Michelle has already dropped off some clothes for him and Elaine and Anna are preparing to visit in the afternoon.

"I have to see him," she says. "I want to go as soon as we can. Will you meet us there?"

Oddly enough, I hadn't confronted the idea of seeing his body. My first reaction is fear. I think immediately of Becky's ex-husband, who died four years ago. We arrived at the hospital just thirty minutes after he had succumbed to a heart attack. We foolishly insisted on seeing him immediately, though the nurses warned us that he hadn't yet been "cleaned up." We weren't prepared for the rawness of it. He lay on a gurney, his head and torso elevated. His skin was gray, his mouth hung open, the plastic intubation tube still protruding, and his eyes bulged, glazed and waxy, fixed in an uncanny stare. Afterward, Bec was unequivocal in saying that she wished she hadn't seen him that way.

What, I now think, can we expect with Oliver? As he is to be cremated, his body is not going to be prepared. And he died not of a heart attack but a gunshot wound to the head. Are we in for one of those Hollywood scenes in which the sheet is pulled back and the loved ones recoil, choked with shock and horror? I fear for Elaine, but I also fear for myself.

I awkwardly try to present some of those hesitations but Elaine is unmovable.

"No," she says firmly. "I have to go. I have to see him. If you don't want to be there, I won't blame you, but I have to be."

It is as if her mother's instincts have risen up in a final, desperate protest. In the face of that ferocity of maternal love, I feel ashamed of my fears, though also find myself unable to dispel them. They are still very much in my mind when we enter the funeral home a few hours later.

As we pass into the building, I'm floating. My legs are moving beneath me, but I'm not walking. I can't help noticing, with absurd attentiveness, the funeral director's failed attempt at a comb-over. How and why, at such a moment of violent extremity, is my mind flooded with such trivia? Am I trying to reattach myself to reality by monitoring such absurd details? I survey the decor of the funeral home as if I am a potential investor in the mortuary business. Once again, my mind is working overtime in an effort to think of anything but the one absolutely unthinkable thing: my son is dead.

*Clouds fascinated him, even as a child. "Look," he would say, not vaguely or dreamily, but with focused intensity: "Aren't they beautiful!" He was a nightmare for the Little League coach. There he would be, standing alone in the outfield. While the rest of the team burst into motion at the crack of a ball on the bat, he would be lost in an upward gaze as if nothing else mattered.*

The four of us enter the room together— Elaine, her sister Ann, Oliver's fiancée Anna, and I. In the far corner, supported by a skirted bier, Oliver lies in the simple gray box that will bear him into the crematory. When we reach the side of the box, the tension in my chest suddenly releases and the tears begin to flow. Miraculously, he lies peacefully with no trace of the wounds that killed him. Aside from the ashen pallor of his skin, he really might be asleep.

Elaine immediately goes to his side and puts her hands on his face, tears streaming down her cheeks but unable to take her eyes off him. None of us can look away. For several minutes we stand silently beside the casket, unable to speak, unable to do anything but gaze at him.

It is in one sense absolutely simple, absolutely elemental. My attention is entirely taken with Oliver's body—his face, his hair, his hands. For many minutes, it is as though nothing else in the world exists. I am deeply grateful to see him, as one might be overcome with relief and happiness to see a child who has been lost and then miraculously found. But at the same time I am repeatedly hammered by the awful truth that snatches him away from me just as he appears to be once again within my grasp. He's dead. He's dead. He's *dead*.

*The door to the jetway is opening now. Surely it will be only moments before we see him. The cast of characters who*

*emerge—the thin man with the gray goatee, the overweight*
*woman who struggles to restrain the loose contents of a*
*brightly flowered canvas bag, the toddler tormenting his*
*parents with obviously theatrical screaming—all suffer*
*from the intensity of my impatience to see Oliver, as if I*
*revenge myself on them for making me wait. Could these*
*people, too, be coming in from Kathmandu? Then, as*
*if by magic, he's there. His chin is obscured by a thin*
*red stubble. His neck is draped with a white, delicately*
*patterned silk scarf, wrinkled and roughly cut. He's*
*wearing the boots we bought together three months ago,*
*now ruddy and almost impossibly worn, and he leans*
*lightly on a simple but vaguely exotic bamboo cane. His*
*sixteen-year-old eyes dance and, try as he might, he's*
*unable to contain the shining beacon of his smile.*

After some time standing together around the
casket, we decide that we will each spend some
time with him by ourselves, something that now,
a little surprisingly, I very much want. I am to
be last, and I mill about in the hallway outside
awaiting my turn, not sure what it will be like to
be alone with him. When I reenter the room, our
encounter initially feels awkward, but it helps that
a chair has been placed next to the casket. Sitting

in that chair affords an unexpected intimacy between us, recalling the hundreds of times that I sat at his bedside when he was a little boy, reading him stories or having one of those heart-to-heart chats that he used to call "our usual talks."

We had not parted on good terms. Less than two months earlier, a scene at his apartment had severely shaken me. When I arrived at the apartment, responding to Elaine's call to say that he was in a serious crisis, I found him not only drunk and high, but armed with two handguns, one holstered on each hip, and a dreadful-looking semiautomatic rifle lying on the couch behind him. It was ten-thirty in the morning. He was watching *Taxi Driver*.

"Oliver, what's going on?" I asked, not sure how quickly or how directly I should ask about the guns. "What's happening?"

I had known for some time that he owned several guns and been horrified by them. Having long ago left behind my adolescent flirtations with guns, few things could have been more foreign and threatening to me. Early on, I tried to be optimistic. His interest in guns and the satisfaction he derived from them were remarkably intense. He several times told me that guns had become the most meaningful thing in his life, something truly his own, something that gave him real joy. Perhaps, I thought hopefully, it could be a good thing. Lots of people have guns as a hobby.

But the scene that now confronted me exceeded my worst fears. For the first time, I felt that I no longer knew this person, that I could not predict what he might do. The whole situation was easily as crazy as anything in *Taxi Driver.*

"Life sucks," he said, not taking his eyes from the television screen.

"Yes, sometimes life sucks," I replied.

"No, Dad, life sucks. Everything sucks. Sometimes I feel like going down to the mall and taking out as many people as I can before the police take me out."

I was momentarily at a loss for words. Stunned and terrified. I had been sick with worry over his deteriorating situation since the fall, when he had been precipitously dropped from the methadone clinic for failing the urine tests and refusing to participate in groups. At the time, he had been flushed with the welcome prospect of getting off methadone. He despised the slavery of the daily cups at the clinic. He hated being an addict. Three months later, after a brief stint in another treatment program that he recklessly dumped, he was in obvious free-fall. But my worry had previously been primarily for him. It now dawned on me with cold horror that he might be a serious danger to other people as well.

Things only got worse. Hearing someone shuffling in the hallway outside the apartment, he drew one of the pistols, leveled it at the door, and pulled back the firing hammer.

"Oliver! What are you doing!?" I blurted out, trying to keep my voice under control. "Jesus, Oliver, put that thing down. Good God, somebody's going to get hurt." He reholstered the gun and casually returned his attention to the TV, as though nothing had happened.

The someone was Anna, and when she came in her manner with him was perfectly natural, as if she had seen all this before, and he seemed fairly good-naturedly to accept her gentle scolding about lying around all morning. In fact, they were quite tender with one another. I began to suspect that the theatrics with the guns had really been a way of poking at my fears and generally messing with me. Anna said that they needed to talk, thanked me for coming over, but suggested that I go. While it made me uneasy to leave the two of them there, I thought perhaps it was better for the moment if I stood aside.

I left confused and deeply alarmed. Afterward I made calls to a lawyer and to the county police, inquiring about what if anything could be done about the guns. I worried that Anna, having lived in the middle of this madness for so long, might have lost the perspective to see it as such. Couldn't we get the guns confiscated, at least until Oliver gets stabilized?

I was told that there was very little that could be done, that Oliver was a legal adult, that he had legal title to the guns, and that gun owners' rights are not easily suspended. Even if we could get a psychiatrist to submit the necessary paperwork, the guns could probably be seized only temporarily. Within a few weeks they'd be back, and then what?

It was my own private collision with the insanity of American gun laws. The response of the policeman I spoke with was basically, "Sorry buddy, we don't like it any better than you do, but our hands are tied." Thinking again of Oliver's mall comment gave me a cold shudder. It's bad enough that the glut of guns in the United States has made suicide by gunshot a national epidemic. But we increasingly seem to be living through another, related epidemic. Call it the Columbine syndrome. People stricken with despair don't just shoot themselves but seem more and more to go out of their way to take as many others with them as possible. On that April day in Colorado, Eric Harris and Dylan Klebold shot thirty-three people, twelve of them fatally.

The idea that my son might be contemplating his own Columbine made me desperately anxious to know about his psychological state. How much risk was there that he might just snap and kill someone? I called to get some advice from the psychiatrist he had seen recently when he registered for suboxone treatment.

It was that phone call that led to the blow-up between us. Insane with cravings and desperate to get back into the suboxone program he'd so blithely abandoned, he called the program only to be told that someone had spoken with me, that the question of guns had come up, and that he was no longer welcome at the clinic. He was furious at my betrayal and, in a blistering barrage of obscenities left on my office phone, he told me so.

That terrible phone message was the last time I heard his voice. No, that's not quite right. It just feels that way. There was one more phone message three weeks later, the apologetic one in which he told me of his last-ditch plan to change his life by joining the army. He wanted to know if I had his social security card.

Now, as I sit beside his coffin, what strikes me most is how quickly the tension melts away, leaving a strangely effortless and deeply welcome feeling of connection with him. Once I start to speak, a steady stream breaks forth. I tell him that I know it hasn't been easy. And I tell him that I forgive him—for the years of friction and ugliness, for his raging addiction, for killing himself. I don't know what was in his mind that night, but I do know that the pressures on him were enormous. I might well have done the same thing in his place. The words come easily and feel incredibly gratifying. I talk to him about how much I respected his decision to have Jack, a decision he fought for with great tenacity when he learned that Anna was pregnant. That resolve took real courage and determination.

I only become really incapacitated by tears when I tell him how much I had missed him during the long, cruel years of his addiction. Barely able to get out the words, I tell him how sorry I am that I couldn't save him, that I fear that I may have been more a part of his problems than any solution to them.

I pause for a time, if only to choke back my own sobbing, then begin to speak about some of the wonderful times we'd had together. I talk of our many trips to Turner, of hiking together in the White Mountains, of canoeing on the Gunpowder River. I remind him of the time, just after his eighth birthday, that the two us drove to the local theater and saw *Dances with Wolves*. It was electrifying for both of us, triggering in him a lifelong love affair with the native peoples of the New World, along with the painful knowledge of their near destruction. When, a few years later, he found on my shelf a book by a Sioux medicine man, *Lame Deer, Seeker of Visions*, he instantly made off with it, reading it cover to cover. His sensitivity to the North American Indian heritage became an important part of the background for his experience of our epic trip to Colorado. That trip was, I tell him, the most completely magical adventure of my life.

As I go on, I find myself chatting with him as if we were sitting on a couple of porch rockers, whiling away an August evening with reminiscences. He remembers, I'm sure, that last night before we left Colorado when we pulled off the road at the peak of Loveland Pass just before sunset and hiked to one of the nearby summits overlooking Denver. We stayed long into the darkening night, watching the canopy of stars come out. They were as brilliant as I'd ever seen them. I was surprised when he wanted me to teach him all the constellations I knew. He kept pressing me to rehearse the names to make sure he'd got them right.

"I didn't know you were so interested in the stars," I said, and I laughed at his answer, wondering if he was fully serious or just baiting my reaction.

"I'm not so interested," he said, "but this is great stuff to smooth chicks with."

I laugh again, sitting beside his dead body. But it is a laugh that dissolves immediately into tears. The sand has run out of some painfully brief hourglass of lightheartedness. He has again withdrawn from me, sunk into the uncanny stillness of death, and I feel myself suddenly and excruciatingly alone. A door that had momentarily opened, allowing me briefly to speak with him, had swung shut. I stand up and look at him, knowing that it will be the last time I ever see his face.

Returning to Elaine's apartment, the images of the Colorado trip are still swirling in my head and I'm delighted when she gives me the thick packet of photographs that Oliver and I took on the trip. I haven't seen them for eight years. Alone at my desk an hour later, I open the packet and it all rushes back to me.

Having pulled off the road and stepped out into the breathless expanse, Oliver wanted to capture the scene with the camera, not just a shot here and there but the whole jaw-dropping sweep of the landscape that surrounded us. He shot half a roll of film, snapping frame by frame in a 360-degree swing. Piecing the pictures together in an image train that stretches from one end of my desk to the other, the magic of the moment again washes over me—its awesome beauty, pregnant with unlimited possibilities, graced by the perfect camaraderie between us.

Then it hits me with an aching wince. Of course, Oliver himself wasn't captured in any of the frames. There sits that funny little rental car, the passenger door still wide open. The slender ribbon of roadway stretches out into the distant flats of grassland, glowing golden in the slanting sunlight. The sea of sage slides toward the jagged contour of the far-off mountains. But there is no trace of the one thing I most want to see.

# 7

I dreamt of Turner last night.

The words don't come easily yet, though the dream is still vivid.

Oncoming winter has left the first bare crust of ice on the pond. The water of the lake underneath is jet black. An inky pool beneath a skim of crystal. The weird thing is that I'm magically able to skate over the thin skin of ice. Gliding over it is intensely exhilarating, though I'm continually aware of the black depth beneath, which fills me with both awe and dread.

I'm fascinated by the dangerous beauty of the black lake, but no words come. The long pause is cramped and pinching.

"Nothing comes to mind?" Barbara asks.

I'm laboring for some association.

*The winter of 1992. He's ten years old. We are on our own for the week as Elaine is visiting a friend in Boston, and Baltimore is paralyzed by a huge ice storm, followed by several days of truly arctic cold. Everything is crusted over by nearly an inch of solid ice, including the local tennis courts, which have become perfect outdoor rinks. Oliver and I take full advantage, skating ecstatically for hours in the numbing cold. For three days in a row, we go out for a session in the morning, come back for a steaming bowl of soup at midday, then go out again in the afternoon and skate until dark.*

*That Saturday, the day before Elaine is due home, we rent a DVD copy of* Back to the Future. *It's another memory I treasure. When the credits roll, we both turn, look each other in the eye, and burst out in unison: "Let's watch it again!"*

Maybe the black water of the dream is my own blackness, the black of my own soul in the wake of his death.

The association feels artificial, unconvincing. Why does this intense dream, with its haunting image of the black lake, leave me so blank?

A second, forgotten part of the dream then flashes into mind unexpectedly. I've come ashore from the icy lake to meet the new owners of the cottage. Upon entering the house, I'm astonished to see that the new tenants have radically changed the place. The kitchen and dining room are gratifyingly unchanged, though I'm amazed when the new owner opens a trap door in the floor of the back kitchen. How could I have missed it? I, of all people, who knew all the secret places?

It's the living room that most astonishes me. The ceiling has been removed to create a lofty, cathedral-like space. Huge, arched windows now line three of the four walls, with smaller windows above. The alcove that housed the old bookcase, the space that yawned open when we threw out the old piano, has been filled by an impressive supporting wall of fieldstone. The wraparound porches, too, have been radically altered, the roofs and screens removed and the decks sanded and varnished. The perimeter is trimmed with a very low railing, a mere marking of the edge that looks out over the lake. And then—totally bizarre—I start crying. Really sobbing.

Immediately upon awakening, my crying in the dream struck me as extremely odd, and in recounting it to Barbara I'm surprised again that I get choked up in the telling of it. There was something powerfully exciting in the dramatic renovations, something that thrilled me, but also something wrenchingly sad. What was the source of that sadness? I have no idea.

However much I had dreaded it beforehand, however horrible I thought it would be, the news of Oliver's death left me utterly broken. As I stood there that night, holding the phone to my ear but no longer knowing what was holding me upright, something absolutely fundamental in myself snapped. I felt like the *Titanic*, having struck an iceberg in the darkness, the hull ripped open below the waterline.

Or maybe the metaphor of an open, gaping wound is all wrong. Maybe it was less a matter of being torn open than of being shut in. Like the sealing of the pyramids. I saw it on the History Channel. At the instruction of the overseer, the activating weight is released. Great blocks of stone, cut with minute precision, slide into their appointed slots far below the surface, sealing off forever the internal passages that interlace the depths of the temple. Is that what has happened inside of me? Am I, too, going to be permanently cut off from the outside world? Cut off from any feeling of happiness? From life itself?

How strange that I have no idea which image is right. Have I been deeply torn open? Are wild currents of emotion now going to rage uncontrolled through my broken soul? Or am I walled up inside myself, a prisoner in a tomb? I can't make sense of it. It feels like both.

The need to know, to make some sense of what happened, that's what drove me into analysis. Yet the labor of the sessions seems impossible. I have to force myself to speak. Why say anything now? What's the point of doing or saying anything?

The idea repeatedly pops into my mind of shooting myself with Oliver's gun. It would close the gap between my inner and outer realities, between feeling outwardly alive and inwardly dead. It would close the gap between him and me. It would be taking his place, an act of deep solidarity with him.

"And this fantasy of shooting yourself, should we be worried about that?" Barbara asks. I have the feeling that she's trying to hide her genuine concern.

I'm quick to answer. No, I'm not really suicidal. But even as I speak the words, I wonder if I am being fully honest, even with myself.

And then another dream flashes into mind, a dream in which I did shoot myself. Even now, these many years later, its details stand out with alarming clarity.

I dreamt it during my second year in college, an especially turbulent time, as I had returned to school after dropping out for a year. It's almost comical to think back on it. I've spent my life in the academy, but when I left after that freshman year I was thinking that I might not come back. My dream of becoming a doctor had somehow deflated, leaving me doubtful that the ivory tower had anything else to offer me. I spent the summer and fall of my year away living on a farm in Connecticut minding horses for a polo enthusiast. Then, after earning some money cutting firewood in Maine, and later working as a painter and wallpaper hanger for a high school friend who had started a little contracting business, I left home with a dear friend and spent the last five months vagabonding around Europe and North Africa.

It was that life-changing trip, exposing me to what felt like a journey to another planet, that convinced me to go back to school. It powerfully struck me at the time and has continued to impress me ever since that it was only when I left the United States and immersed myself for an extended period in a string of foreign countries that I realized how very little I knew about anything. About art and architecture, about history and literature, about politics and the social order. It took going abroad to realize that I was an idiot.

The initial premise of the dream, the sort of thing that you just know, was taken from Camus's novel *The Plague*, which I had read that summer. The background premise was that everyone, absolutely everyone, was going to die of the coming scourge.

I'm in a room on the second story of a large house, apparently my family's house, a classically European place with high ceilings and big mirrors. There is a lot of commotion. The family is preparing to leave. Outside, trunks and boxes are being loaded into carts. Inside, furniture that can't be taken is being draped with white sheets.

All this activity strikes me as pointless. If the plague will eventually kill everyone, then why bother to cover the furniture? Why leave the house at all? Surrounded by all these absurd efforts, I resolve to kill myself. In the moment it seems perfectly rational.

I vividly remember the cool, black steel of the revolver, its heft as I turn it over in my hands with peculiar fascination. The most electrifying moment comes just after I put the barrel of the gun into my mouth and pull the trigger. The gun goes off, firing a slug up into the back my head. *But I don't die.* I'm exquisitely, horribly aware that the bullet has ripped through the soft tissue of my brain, leaving a trail of injury that can never be repaired. And yet I'm still fully conscious, still fully alive.

My stomach muscles have tightened. I feel cramped and claustrophobic. It's hard to get my breath. Barbara says nothing to relieve the silence. I have to keep talking, if only to escape it.

Still alive—it's comical in a black sort of way. I find myself getting angry. How can I not be dead? It's as maddening as it is crazy. In a heat of irritation I again resolve to kill myself. In quick succession, I fire all the remaining bullets into my head. But the result is the same. I'm still alive. I'm horribly wounded, in fact far more so than before, but I'm still alive.

l woke up drenched in sweat and stumbled around, shaken for the rest of the day. Even now, the dream stands out as unique, no doubt the weirdest, most devastating dream of my life.

Barbara stills says nothing, and for a moment I find myself flushed with anger. How could she not offer some sympathetic comment?

Then it hits me—good God!—Oliver, too, shot himself in the head. Two times, separated by three decades, a bullet in the head. The moment of his pulling the trigger again flashes, now with an insanely redoubled sense of horror. My dream seems to be more than a premonition. It is as if I dreamed my son's death thirty years before the fact.

My fingers are tingling and the back of my neck feels hot against the pillow. I twist restlessly, unable to find a comfortable position. I'm a wriggling insect pinned to a scrap of cardboard.

The anguish over an act that can't be undone, that's the central thing. It's the sense of

something irreparably broken—the bullet
having torn its way through my brain, yet
without killing me. Thinking back on it now,
the dream seems less about hopelessness (that
everyone would die of the plague) or about a
self-destructive impulse (shooting myself) than
about regret over an act whose consequences
cannot be undone.

I've always had a dread of things just like that, of
being helpless to undo the irretrievable consequences
of a stupid mistake. I've even connected it with
suicide. It sounds bizarre—confessing it embarrasses
me—I've often imagined with special horror the
idea of making a suicidal jump from a tall building,
then regretting it in midair.

Barbara still says nothing and again her silence
rankles. She offers no consolation, no shred
of sympathetic understanding. Nothing. I'm
tortured by her silence. And suddenly—I can't
help myself—I hate her for it.

I think that's why I've always felt a strange
sympathy with certain criminals.

It's a stupid, irrelevant digression, but I go on.

It's about people who wreck their lives with some terrible mistake and are condemned to regret it forever. Like that story in the news some years ago about a young woman who drowned her two young children. Susan Smith. She ended up on the cover of *Time*. I actually saved the issue. She locked her kids in the car and rolled it into a pond, then told the police they'd been abducted. Her motive, she said, was her fear of losing her boyfriend. He wanted nothing to do with children, or so she imagined.

Everyone was outraged by her, of course. The ultimate bad mother. The crowd clamored for the death penalty, but I could only feel sorry for her. What an infinitude of regret must now and forever consume her!

Like me? Yes, like me!

I'm suddenly and unexpectedly cornered by the drift of my own thoughts. I've known all along that I would have to talk about it. I can't avoid it any longer.

The truth is that I feel Oliver's death was my fault. I spit out the words.

Barbara is still silent, but I anticipate a response and cut it off before she can say anything.

I know very well that not every kid whose parents get divorced ends up killing himself. Rebecca never tires of trying to get me to believe it. But it was Oliver's discovery of a casual dalliance of mine that led to my break with Elaine.

It was early September of his senior year. He came home from school unexpectedly just after noon. I was in the house with my viola partner, Christine, a woman a little older than me. Her marriage was even more unhappy than mine. Over the preceding few months, we had gotten sexually involved.

Appearances were mostly innocent when Oliver found us together. Our instrument cases lay open in the living room beside the music stands, though we weren't playing at the moment. He said nothing at the time, but I suspected that he drew the right conclusions. For my part, feeling discovered by him led to a real crisis. I might easily have worked up a cover story—shamefully enough, I think I might have if it had been Elaine who walked in—but lying to Oliver felt out of the question.

When Elaine arrived home, the three of us sat down and I told them the truth. Elaine listened, stiff and obviously deeply pained, but mostly silent. She had known since the spring that this moment was coming. I told her how unhappy I was and that I wanted to leave, but when she pressed me to postpone it, I agreed to stay together at least until Oliver graduated from high school. She asked what I wanted to do now. I said that I thought that I should move out of the house, at least for some period of time. She turned to Oliver and asked him what he thought should happen. He, too, seemed amazingly calm and quiet. Sullen, but calm. He simply said that he agreed with me. I should leave.

Of course, I was afraid of what this turn of events might mean for him. Afraid above all that he might feel that he was the cause of the breakup. I told him that evening, and repeated it several times later on, that his mother and I had long-standing problems that had nothing to do with him and that he wasn't in any way responsible for what had happened. I even told him that I had confessed to his mom about another love affair some years earlier, after which she and I had gone into a long period of couples counseling.

Barbara has still said nothing and the silence weighs on me, a cold, gray stone. I'm regretting ever having gotten into this analysis.

I begin to expand on the story—the intractable impasses in my marriage, my confused and guilty sense of something missing in our relationship, the multiple stints of counseling that I dragged us into—but the more I talk, the sicker I feel. It is a complicated story that I want desperately to render accurately. But I also feel like I'm making excuses for myself. To whom could such excuses be convincing?

# 8

Waking up on Wednesday, the demon is upon me immediately. It shoots through me, a now-familiar, cold electricity. I, too, am lying in that dull gray box, squeezed on all sides, unable to move. I hear a ghostly echo of my own voice asking if there isn't some way back to life as it was.

*His face comes to me with astonishing vividness. I see his smile, that wry, half smile so typical of him, the one he tries to conceal with a slight inclination of his head. I can see the steely blue of his eyes as he looks up at me. The red stubble on his chin stands out with perfect clarity. He is wearing that heavy, oatmeal-colored sweater with the red-and-green stripe across the chest. It's like he's standing right in front of me. No, it's more than that. He is more real than real, present with an uncanny and impossible intensity.*

Everything I ever expected about the experience of death is upside down. He's dead, but in death memories of him assume shocking force. Their intensity is all the more arresting because I feel myself to be so utterly drained and empty. I often have the sense of being invisible to other people, as if they might cast a glance in my direction and miss me altogether. Yet in his absence, Oliver seems—impossibly, unthinkably—more vividly present than ever before. I am the one who is dead. I am the one who has been reduced to something vacant, barren, annihilated.

How could anyone who's suffered a really bad death have gotten this wrong? How and why did we ever come up with the idea that the departed become empty specters—"ghosts"? On the contrary, stolen from us by death, our loved ones become incomparably more vibrant to memory and imagination, in a weird way even more insistently real than they were when they were alive. If we are haunted by them, it is for being oppressed, not by their absence, but by their excessive presence. It is we, the survivors, who are deprived of reality. Depleted by the anemia of grief, it is we who become ghosts.

There seems to me only one solution to this riddle: we style the dead as empty phantoms in a desperate attempt to turn the tables, to saddle the dead with the very void of reality that we ourselves have become. We think of the dead as wispy nothings in order to convince ourselves that we have survived losing them, that we can still stand up, that we still exist.

Also among the stranger effects of Oliver's death has been a general catastrophe of memory. If some recollections of him are superanimated, other banks of recall seem to have been blasted and erased altogether. The trauma of his death has washed through my memory like a mental tsunami, sweeping away things that aren't firmly buckled down, while leaving other, more significant memories standing, now all the more prominent for being stripped of everything surrounding them.

But it's not only my memory that has been knocked off its foundations. I find myself in a constant state of low-grade delirium. I continually have the sensation of floating—yes, exactly like a ghost. The feeling of my own weightlessness is matched by a general sense of the unreality of everything outside of me. All colors are reduced to gray. Sounds seem strangely muffled, as they are during a heavy snowstorm. I continually have the impression of having awoken midway through a movie whose plot I no longer understand.

In the midmorning, I decide to visit my office. There is no real need for me to be there, as I have canceled my classes for the week, but I make ready to go as if mindlessly clinging to a routine, or maybe just wishing I could be saved by one. Arriving at the Humanities Building, I immediately regret having made the trip, mostly as I begin to dread running into colleagues and having to explain what has happened. I don't want to hear their condolences. I grab the mail, stuff it into my bag without looking at it, and leave, hoping to get away unnoticed.

As I walk back to my car, parked just beside the reservoir off Cold Spring Lane, a beat-up gray Nissan pulls up beside me. The window rolls

down on the passenger's side close to me and I
have to lean over to see the driver, a man in his
early thirties.

"You need a ride anywhere?" he asks.

My first impulse is to think that this is
someone who knows me and whose name, in my
fog of grief and fatigue, I have forgotten. Does he
know what's happened? I thrash my memory. Is
he someone who works at the university?

"No, my car's right over there. But thanks." I
turn to walk away but he speaks again.

"Hey."

I turn back. He is leaning across the front seat
in my direction, as if to emphasize his desire to
talk to me. I am by now pretty sure that I don't
know him, but my inclination to ignore him is
checked by a single thought that jumps powerfully
to mind: Oliver would talk to him. Oliver always
had a wonderful openness to strangers, especially
toward the down-and-outers with whom he had
an easy, charming manner that I respected and
even envied. I should give this guy a chance.

"What are you doing today?" he asks.

The intrusiveness of the question annoys me
and while I try to be civil, my answer is curt.
"Actually, I'm planning my son's funeral."

There is a pause in which he appears to be at a loss for a response. Perhaps he is trying to reckon whether I am being honest with him or just trying to get rid of him. I again begin to turn away and he again calls me back.

"Hey, do you live nearby? Is anyone home?"

At this point, my sense of irritation intensifies, but in the moment I can't make sense of his question and conclude—ludicrously, as it turned out—that he is asking about my home out of sympathy, that he is concerned that my family is there to support me in my time of grief, etc.

"Yeah, I live just a couple of miles from here, and, yeah, my family's there. I'm okay, thanks."

I think with some relief that this is the end of our little interview and begin to turn away but he once more calls me back.

"Hey," he says, pausing until I turn around to face him a last time. "You want some head?"

I answer with completely restrained politeness, as though he had asked me if I was in need of directions.

"No thanks, I'm fine. I'm okay, thanks."

Even after the words have left my mouth it takes me another second to absorb the strangeness and comedy of the situation, whereupon I feel for the first time a wave of fear. Who the hell is this guy? What does he really want? Is he dangerous?

I begin walking briskly away, resolved not to have anything further to do with him. But there is still some distance between me and my car and out of the corner of my eye I can see that he is circling around to intersect my path. Oh God, what does he want now? Have I offended him? Is he going to try to mug me?

Sure enough, as I reach my car, he has pulled up beside me. I brace myself for the worst. The window rolls down again.

"I'm sorry about your son," he says.

I am caught up short by this unexpected expression of sympathy and feel silly and embarrassed to have been afraid of him only a moment before. I mumble a thank-you and begin to get in my car, but not without feeling the whole catastrophe of Oliver's death return with renewed force. Watching the gray car drive off I have the feeling of being a stranger in the world, the feeling that however off-beat this guy is, whatever he's into, I'm even more of a misfit, a displaced and shattered shell of a person, a refugee.

When I get home, still struck by the weirdness of the whole episode, I tell the story to Rebecca,

who doesn't hesitate to conclude that the man
was trying to get money for a fix. The possibility
hadn't even occurred to me. For some reason,
I had taken everything he said at face value,
including his final proposition. I had assumed
that he was just interested in sex, that sucking
off strangers just happened to be his thing. But I
know very well that drug addiction, and heroin
addiction in particular, is rampant in the city of
Baltimore. We're the American capital of heroin
distribution. In 2006, when Oliver died, it was
purer, cheaper, and more readily available here
than anywhere in the country. The statistics are
appalling. Almost one in every ten inhabitants
were active drug addicts. Of those, 48,000 were
addicted to heroin. And I knew the depths to
which most addicts are driven in the desperate
struggle to support their habit. My own son spent
the last four years of his life as a heroin addict.
Perhaps it was the pain of that very knowledge
that kept me from thinking about it.

*It was after midnight when the call came from Mt. Sinai*
*Hospital. Barely conscious, his body had been delivered*
*there by the police. He'd apparently been downtown trying*
*to score some drugs and ran afoul of a gang of kids who*

*held him down and savagely beat and kicked him. When*
*we get to his room his bloodied face is swollen to grotesque*
*proportions. His eyes are reduced to greasy slits above his*
*puffed-out cheeks. His lips, massive and deep purple, are*
*horribly split open. He looks like a bruised and battered*
*jack-o'-lantern. He can neither move nor speak but when*
*he sees us, his bruises run wet with tears.*

How many other torments had he suffered that I
know nothing about?

Early in the afternoon, Anna calls. She is heading
over to get some things at the apartment that she
and Oliver shared and doesn't want to be there
alone. I am happy to keep her company, but also
want to see the apartment for myself. Though I
am apprehensive about what I might find there, I
have to see the spot where he died.

Arriving at the apartment I am shocked by
the yellow police tape across the door. It salts my
already open wound to think of the place as a
crime scene. The commotion of a few nights ago
plays in my mind like a movie scene—the flashing
lights of the police cars and the ambulance, the
alarmed neighbors standing around, the gurney

being wheeled out. When I see Anna's car round the corner and the prospect of going in becomes more immediate, I shiver. It isn't just a matter of my growing fear about the bloody spectacle that awaits us in the apartment but the brute reality of Oliver's death. I am still learning one of the most basic lessons of mourning. Against all logic, the weight of grief that already seems infinite in the first encounter with death becomes with time, in wave after awful wave, ever more crushing.

It helps me to see Anna tear aside the crime scene tape with perfect matter-of-factness, as if I hope some of her composure will rub off on me, but when we enter the apartment it immediately becomes clear that she isn't ready to go into the bedroom where Oliver shot himself. We sit in the living room for more than an hour, talking over a continual chain of cigarettes. It is the first time that I've had a chance to ask her in detail about what happened that night.

"He'd been bad all day," she says. "He was high when I came home and I knew it was going to be a bad night. When he went into the bathroom and locked the door, I really lost it. I told him to open the door, that I knew he was shooting up, and that I wasn't putting up with it anymore. I told him I was going to break down the door if he didn't open it. He finally came out, yelling at me about accusing him all the time. He stormed around the house, slamming things and yelling. Then he went into the kitchen and started cooking some bacon. When Jack came up to him and asked if he could have some, Oliver yelled at him, too. He was completely out of his mind."

It is especially excruciating to think of little Jack in tears, frightened by seeing his parents fighting again, and unable to understand why his father was yelling at him. But I also know how much Oliver loved Jack. More than anything in the world. I know that when he cooled off after an outburst, the greatest pain was always his regret over having failed his son.

"Later," Anna goes on, "after Jack had gone to bed, Oliver was sitting in the living room and I started to talk to him about what we were going to do. I told him I was really at the end of my rope. I told him what you and I talked about, about how if he wanted to stay in the apartment, he needed to go to the group meetings at the clinic, that he needed to keep the guns in the safe, and that he couldn't have drugs in the house. Then I told him that I had filed a notice of eviction and I showed him the paper. I told him that it meant that he had thirty days to get his act together or he was going to have to find someplace else to live. It wasn't like I was telling him that he had to get over all his problems in a month. Just that he needed to meet those minimal conditions if he wanted to keep living here."

Anna pauses and takes a long drag on her cigarette.

"Well, he pretty much freaked out. He stood up and started pacing around. He couldn't believe that I was going to evict him. He had heard me talk about it, but he didn't think I would actually do it. He turned to me and said, 'Let me get this straight. I have thirty days, and then I'm out.' I tried to explain again what I needed him to do, that if he agreed to stop using in the house and get into treatment then he could stay, that I wanted him to stay, but it didn't seem to register with him.

"A few days earlier we'd had a really good talk. It was one of those talks when he really listened and really connected with me. He cried and cried, and he told me that he really wanted to get straight. He told me that he'd do anything to get his life back again. He said he knew that it was really hurting me and Jack, and that he was going to do whatever it took. As he stood there in front of me, I asked him whether that talk had meant anything to him. He started to walk away, but turned and looked back at me. 'It meant more to me than you'll ever know,' he said. Then he just went into the bedroom and closed the door.

"After a couple of minutes I heard a sound. Like a pop. It wasn't very loud. Jack didn't even wake up. Anyway, I didn't know what it was and I got up and knocked on the door and there was no answer. I tried to open the door but it was locked. Then I started getting scared and I called his name really loud, but he didn't answer. So I pushed against the door until it broke open and he was lying on the bed with blood all over the place. There was so much blood. You wouldn't believe how much blood there was."

She stops talking for a while and just sits smoking. She looks at the floor, pulling herself together to get the rest of it out.

"I called 911 and told them that he had shot himself and the woman asked me if he was still alive, if he was still breathing, and I said I didn't know. When I first went in the bedroom, he actually made some sounds, like gurgling or something, but I didn't think he was still alive. The woman said that I should do CPR. I told her that I thought he was dead, but she kept insisting that I do CPR. She just kept saying that I had to do that, so I did. But when I tried to lift his head, when I put my hand back there, behind his head, it was like there was nothing there. I got blood all over me. When the police came, my shirt was completely soaked. One of the policemen had to go into the room and get me another shirt. I couldn't go in there again."

"What a blessing that Jack didn't wake up. It's incredible, really. Wasn't he right in the next room?"

"Yeah, but Oliver used a pillow to muffle it. That's part of what Michelle and John had to clean up. Blood and pillow stuffing got blown all over the place."

"He used a pillow? You mean he covered the gun and shot through a pillow?"

"Yeah, you didn't know that?"

I hadn't known it, and it suddenly answers a whole series of agonizing questions. It definitely wasn't an accident, then. He couldn't have been distractedly toying with the gun. His death wasn't the result of any half-formed intention.

"So he clearly meant to kill himself."

Anna takes another long pull on her cigarette and exhales slowly. "Yeah."

I lean over and hug her. "I'm so sorry, Anna. I'm so sorry. It must have been terrible for you. No one should have to go through something like that." The scene she described keeps filling out in my mind in all its horror.

"You must know that it wasn't your fault, Anna," I say. "I'm the one who told you that you had to evict him. You had to do that. Nothing else was working. Nobody could have predicted that he would shoot himself over it."

Actually, Elaine predicted it. When she learned of the plan to serve him with an eviction notice she had called me to express her concern about it. She was clearly worried about what it might do to him. I was worried, too. I knew that he might take it very badly and that, in the extreme case, there was a chance that it might push him over the edge. But I was convinced that putting some pressure on him was the only chance we had for helping him get into treatment. I thought that having a deadline thirty days away would be a motivation, and that he would have time to adjust. And if he couldn't handle that pressure now, wouldn't it only be harder to deal with later?

"You suffered long and hard with him, Anna. You did everything you could for him. I know that. If there is anyone to blame, it's me. I knew that the eviction threat was risky, and I pushed you to do it anyway."

Again we sit for a long time in silence. It is she who gets up first. She has other things she has to do. She will take the things she needs and be on her way. I tell her I want to stay longer and that I'll close the door behind me. After collecting the things she came for, mostly clothes for Jack and herself, she hugs me goodbye and leaves me alone.

Sitting now by myself on the couch, the silence of the place closes in on me and I suddenly and very powerfully feel Oliver's presence. It is another moment of strange intimacy with him. Despite my grief, a deep calm falls over me. I no longer feel the slightest trace of fear or apprehension. I snuff out my last cigarette, get up from the couch, and walk into the bedroom where he died.

Oliver and Anna slept on a queen-sized mattress laid on the floor. The bedclothes have been stripped from it and stuffed into three or four plastic bags that stand beside the bureau. The shades at the window are closed and the room is dimly lit but there is no mistaking the enormous bloodstain that spreads across the naked mattress. Seeing it makes me choke for a moment with the impulse to cry, but no tears come. As if by mindless instinct, I immediately kneel down and put my hands on the stain, now dried and stiff. The curious calm deepens. I feel that I am putting my hands on him, that this dried blood is the last vestige of him. As I sit down on the mattress, still with my hands on the stained material, stroking back and forth, I feel as if we are sitting there together. I say nothing aloud, but it feels like we engage in a long and tender conversation.

Once again, as has happened repeatedly over the preceding couple of days, whatever expectations I had in advance are utterly contradicted by my experience. Having feared this moment, unsure exactly what I would feel but convinced that it would be somehow traumatic,

I'm unexpectedly embraced by a remarkable stillness. Strangest of all, I feel absolutely connected to him.

Before leaving, I rummage a bit through the bedside table. He had left a barely legible scribble of goodbye to Anna the night he killed himself, but nothing that rose to the level of a suicide note, certainly nothing that gave the slightest indication of what was in his mind. The hope springs up in me that he might perhaps have left something else. It is painful to find nothing, but even more painful to realize, as my search exhausts itself, that I am really looking for something that might be addressed to me. The selfishness of my motive embarrasses me but I cannot avoid being wounded by the thought that when he shot himself, his mind was entirely taken up with things and people other than me.

In one of the drawers there are a couple of notebooks in which he had kept journals and drawings. I tuck them under my arm when I leave and later that evening, in the silence of my study, I spend several hours poring over them. I am again impressed, as I'd often been in the past, with both his drawings and his writing. The drawings are strikingly original. Graceful, economical, done with a sure eye for line. A number of them, still lifes and drawings of Anna, are arrestingly beautiful. His writing, too, is clear and clean. The prose is simply wrought to express his thoughts directly, yet deeply evocative.

Many of the drawings and journal entries are explicitly about drugs. He speaks about how much he hated them, and how much he hated himself for being their slave. The following entry was written sometime in 2004, two years before his death.

*Why I want my life to be different*

*Over the years I have made many mistakes. Well, most people would consider them mistakes, anyway. My decisions and actions fueled a disease that at one time lay dormant somewhere in my body. As I began to use drugs the disease rapidly grew out of control. As a result I suffered a great deal and caused everyone who loved me a great deal of pain and worry.*

*Today looking back I am horrified at the destructive things I've done, the dangers involved, and the problems I have caused myself and others around me. However, I don't regret anything I did and would not go back and change anything if I could. All aspects of my past make up who I am today and I like myself enough to dismiss all regrets.*

*However, I do not want to live life the same way anymore. I'm sick of hurting myself and I'm really sick of hurting other people. I'm sick of breaking promises and my own set of values. I'm sick of blowing all my money on something that eventually comes out in my piss. I'm sick of waking up ten times a night to check outside for cops. I'm sick of lying. I'm sick of stealing. I'm sick of having nothing to be proud of. I'm sick of trading in my dreams for dope. I'm sick of being worried about going to jail. I'm sick of worrying about overdosing. I'm sick of worrying about means to get drugs. I'm sick of needing drugs to get out of bed in the morning. I'm sick of worrying if my needles are clean. I'm sick of scheming day and night, and I'm sick and tired of revolving every little aspect of my life around drugs of some kind. As I've heard people say, "I'm sick and tired of being sick and tired." So, I guess the answer to the question at hand is I'm sick of the way things were and hopeful and confident about the way things will be.*

Also in the journal is a letter to Anna. For a moment, I wonder whether the prose is the work of someone else that he has copied into his journal. But, no, they're his own words. It's my son's voice.

*The earth is in constant flight. Orbiting the sun in a never-ending cipher of planets. Driven by a mysterious energy and an endless surplus of momentum this phenomenon has been relentless since an age unimaginable, and will continue till the end of time. This endless pattern births many others, all around us, set in their ways and motions. The seasons, sunrises and sunsets, the tides, the phases of the moon, and night and day are all spawned from this powerful energy that moves the planets but eludes our senses with the absence of physical properties. I speak now of this energy because it is like my love for you. My love for you is not something you can see, taste, hear, or touch. It is mysterious. Undefinable. Immeasurable. Never-ending. It is an energy which powers and directs something far greater. My life. My love for you has changed my life. It influences my decisions, dictates my mood, brings hope and fear, joy and sorrow, tears and smiles, pleasure and pain. My love for you gives me balance, a foundation, security. It puts everything in place, letting me see where I am, what I want, what I have, where I'm going, where I was, where I want to be and who I am. The love I have for you keeps me going and keeps me growing. It sheds light into the darkness. My love for you has changed my life in so many wonderful ways. It has made me what I am today.*

*You are the most beautiful, amazing, and precious person I have ever known. Every detail of your body, your being, your spirit, your essence, has thrown me into the most wonderful place I will ever be. Here and now, in love with you.*

# 9

How could anyone keep this up for very long?
I am chronically uncomfortable on the couch.
Working myself up to speak feels like sticking a
finger down my throat.

My thoughts turn again to memories of Turner. Is
this just more distraction? I begin to talk about the
happy intimacy between my younger sister and
me, about the untold hours we spent wandering
along the beach toward "the Point," a long spit
of sand at the north end of the cove that projects

out into the middle of the lake. We would pick blueberries along the way, then bask in the sun-warmed shallows, though we never dared go too far. The sand finger terminates farther out in an underwater cliff that we referred to in hushed tones as "the Drop-off."

We played natives on the pine-needle floor of the woods, taking turns being the helpless captive of bloodthirsty cannibals eager to torture their meal before eating it. The victim's body had to be rubbed all over with burning mustard. Innocent as it was at the time, almost comical now to remember, it was a first stirring of my sexuality.

Is it touching on the issue of sex that suddenly makes me feel self-conscious? Is it my comment, appended to the memories of my sister, that her name, too, is Barbara? No, it's talking about Turner in general. I felt a similar hesitation before, a vague sense of an illicit pleasure taken in recalling those memories. Savoring those enjoyments in the wake of Oliver's death feels almost criminal.

"Thinking about Turner now feels like an escape," Barbara says.

Yes, of course. It's an escape. In some ways I've been escaping all my life. That's what the idyllic times with my sister were—escaping some work project that my father, grandfather, and brother were sweating out. My sister was my original partner in crime.

The thought of the work at Turner brings a wince. In my high school years, my attitude changed and I often helped my father in working around the place. But in my childhood I detested it. Or maybe it was more a matter of detesting my brother for being so eager for it. It disgusted me that he would go to any lengths to win approval. I hated it when he would bring home his school report card like a trophy and trumpet his high grades. In the face of all that self-promotion, I ran the other way. I remember once deliberately hiding my own report card, stuffing it into the stack of magazines on the coffee table. My grades were good enough. It was the clawing for recognition that I couldn't stand.

The adventures with my sister were an escape from all that. But even more frequently I would escape by myself. Out into the woods, but especially out on the lake. My greatest joy was slipping along the wooded shoreline, alone in the old cedar-ribbed canoe. It was in those years that hunting for turtles became an obsession. Fishing, too. The early mornings were the best times, when the surface of the lake was mirror-calm and clouds of mist hung over the water like a wispy garment shed by the retreating darkness. I was often gone well before sunup, before anyone else in the house was stirring, and would return only when the clink of the breakfast dishes could be heard distantly across the glassy water.

I always felt at a distance from my family, the odd one, the misfit. With an older brother and a younger sister, I fell between the cracks of my parents' attentions. Even at the main house in Cumberland, I felt more at home in the woods. And what beautiful woods they were! Gently rolling ground on the forest floor, carpeted with ferns and mosses, canopied overhead by great pines and hemlocks.

It wasn't for nothing that my best friend in grade school, Jimmy Wheaton, lived a half mile's walk through the woods in back of our house. Those woods were our kingdom. We could run the paths in the dark and knew all the best places—the wild blackberry patch, the frog pond, rock ledges for climbing, and groves of hemlock saplings that we used for swinging, climbing to the top until the trees bent and swooped, setting us down like parachutists. In winter, we skated on the pond until our cheeks stung and our hands ached with cold.

I loved our adventures at the ocean. Racing along the great skirt of jumbled rock at the water's edge where a misstep would kill you. Sitting for long stretches beside the still tide pools, enchanted by the tiny creatures crawling among the barnacles. We combed the tangle of seaweed at the high-tide line for the pale and ghostly shells of baby horseshoe crabs. I remember a February deep freeze when we crossed one of the smaller coves on "rubber ice," black and squeaking under our weight.

Is that the memory that came back in my dream of the black lake?

Jimmy Wheaton was an unusual kid, with an off-beat sense of things. When we made up a language of our own—my brother mocked me for it—it was Jimmy who was its real author. When we sailed one of my ship models in the stream between our houses, it was Jimmy who thought of setting it on fire. The plastic masts and hull sputtered gloriously with tiny flames and spewed convincing mini-clouds of black smoke.

Jimmy Wheaton also killed himself. In his early forties he jumped off the South Portland bridge.

It's out of my mouth before I know it. I had been carried away on the trail of memories, unaware of the parallel. My only child and my best friend in childhood both killed themselves. Nor is the likeness limited to their suicides. Jimmy, too, struggled all his adult life with substance abuse, both drugs and alcohol.

Things fell apart between us in the seventh grade. The magic candle that had lit our little world went out. I don't know why. Not long after he began a steadily accelerating cycle of drug use. By the time we were in high school, I had lost track of him pretty completely.

I loved his genius for finding secret passages to other realms. He was a door to something outside my family, something decidedly *not* my family. It was a door I was well accustomed to passing through. In the rear corner of the house lot in Cumberland, on somewhat higher ground and just at the forest's edge, stood a magnificent hemlock. I used to climb that tree and perch myself in the uppermost branches, then look back at the house, perfectly framed by the boughs. It was like sitting on the shoulders of a sympathetic giant. On the very midline between the house and the woods, it was a point of self-imposed exile from which I could look down from a splendid distance. In many ways I'm still up there, by myself.

"In many ways?" she says in the pause.

Yes, in one way or another, I always feel at a distance from people. I had a childhood mania for building forts in the woods. I built several treehouses, the last of which was an enormous affair, a half mile or more out in the woods, built with scrap lumber some buddies and I stole from nearby houses under construction. It was cornered on four large trees, and it was high up. It had three windows with hinged shutters and a tar-papered roof. When I was in high school, long after my own interest in it had faded, "The Treehouse" became a notorious hangout for teen-aged, beer-drinking miscreants.

Or the sailboat. My forty-year-old Alberg 30. Nothing fancy but just big enough for a decent offshore passage. What's that but another treehouse? I love its self-sufficiency. There is nothing so sweet as having fully provisioned it for a cruise, with everything I need tucked away. It's nice to have other people aboard sometimes, but I'm happiest when I'm sailing alone. The self-steering vane, the mechanical gizmo on the stern that minds the course once it's adjusted, allows me to sail for hours without touching the tiller. I love the two days' offshore voyage from Cape May to Block Island—it's the anxious pleasure of simply being far out, a speck in the big blue, with the sun setting at night, rising in the morning, and then setting again on 360 degrees of uninterrupted ocean.

My attraction to the isolation of single-handed sailing—it reminds me of my thing about *Lawrence of Arabia*. I was eight when my parents took us to see it. July 1962. It's hard to overstate its impact on me. On the way home from the theater, we had to pull over so I could throw up. Seeing it a second time twelve years later as an undergraduate, the frames unfolded with shock after shock of perfect recognition.

The final image of the film gives me a chill. The empty look on Lawrence's face when his driver asks him about "goin' 'ome." I've always identified with that loneliness. When I was in graduate school and immersed in my dissertation, I revisited the Lawrence obsession, reading *The Seven Pillars of Wisdom* and his other works, along with several biographies. John Mack's book *A Prince of Our Disorder*—maybe you know it?—it's a broadly psychoanalytic study of Lawrence.

It feels like key elements of my life are lining up like so many beads on a single thread. All these years, it feels like I've been in that tree-sitter's position, casting a distant eye on my family home. Doesn't that position of exile exactly describe my penchant for philosophy? My spot in the hemlock tree could be a good shorthand for the original meaning of the Greek word *theoria* ("theory"). It means seeing from a distance, as from a high point that surveys a field below. I apparently started philosophizing, or something like it, at a very early age.

Is the pattern of my life reducible to this grossly simple form? In a deep sense, it seems that I have never left my hemlock tree. Looking astern at the receding lights of Cape May, I am still in that old canoe at Turner looking back at the cottage. Am I so completely stuck in the same repetition?

In the silence, I indulge a sidebar reflection. How much are other people pinned to similar patterns? Of course, we like to think of ourselves as free of such things. But what if we fancy ourselves to be spontaneous, unpredictable, capable of anything, precisely because we're not?

I'm laughing to realize it. In struggling to absorb a lesson about the deep root of my own disposition to philosophy, I am already back at it. I'm spinning a little web of theory.

But then—the conclusion is forcing itself on me—I have to revise my whole idea of my childhood. I've always thought of it as exceptionally happy. That happy childhood has always been a kind of article of faith, a part of what I've always taken for granted and even felt deeply grateful for. And it was my lonesome sense of beauty that certified that youthful happiness, like a guarantee of pure gold. A childhood saturated with that much beauty must have been happy.

And yet—it suddenly seems obvious—being monarch of one's own little kingdom, however beautiful, isn't the same as being happy.

# *10*

Elaine's apartment has been the base of
operations all week. By Thursday morning,
the place feels like a sort of crisis center,
with constant phone calls, checklists of to-dos
cluttering the kitchen table, people shuttling to
and from the airport and doing errands, little
groups on the porch smoking and talking in
murmurs. I am secretly happy this morning to
have a few hours of solitude in my study at home,
alone with my thoughts.

The better part of a year ago, I compiled a history of Oliver's drug use and treatment as background for an addiction counselor. I now pull it from the file drawer and scan its contents.

Aside from the sheer length of this list of agonies, covering more than eight years, one of the things that jumps out at me is the month of March. So many times he had crises in March: blowups, overdoses, fights, run-ins with the police. His first suicide attempt was in March, three years before the one that finally killed him. But even more striking is the number of times that Oliver refused treatment. I cannot help thinking that this, more than anything else, is what did him in. He repeatedly rejected all forms of therapy or counseling. It was refusing to attend the group meetings at the methadone clinic that got him kicked out of the program and led to his final crisis. Why was he so stubbornly resistant?

The thought of his bullheaded nature brings with it a pang of annoyance, one of the few hints of anger that I've felt toward him since his death. It was that stubbornness, that unwillingness to listen to anyone else's advice or to lean on anyone else's help, that led him to break off the suboxone treatment with which he'd hoped to compensate for getting dropped from the methadone program. The clinic people told him, we all told him, that he was setting himself up for disaster. But he couldn't be budged. He was going to go it alone.

However maddening that streak of mulelike intractability, and however much it was a liability to him, I was also tempted to admire it. I saw it come out most intensely when Anna was pregnant with Jack.

I well remember the night he told me about it. I learned later that he had already broken the news to Elaine, who was inclined to think it might be a good thing, hoping that it might rally and focus him with the force of necessity. I was initially very negative on the whole idea, as I thought any practical-minded person should be. He was nineteen years old, had no education beyond high school and no employable skill, and he was struggling with a serious drug problem. But he rejected my cautions. No doubt he had anticipated my resistance and was prepared to meet it. He seemed energized by a force of resolve more powerful than anything I had ever seen before.

"That's it, Dad," he said with gentle but unmovable firmness. "Anna's pregnant and we're going to have a child together. That's what's happening."

"But you've got to know that this isn't like buying a car, Oliver," I began. "This isn't even like deciding to get married. You might later decide to sell the car, or even end the marriage, but this is a decision that is absolutely for life. Once you have a child, you're that child's father forever."

"That's exactly the point, Dad," he said immediately. "I already am this child's father."

Up until that moment, I had been assuming that ending the pregnancy was at least a possibility, and it now dawned on me that, in Oliver's mind at least, an abortion was out of the question. The fierceness of his response caught me by surprise.

In the pause that followed, I couldn't help feeling that my own argument had already been defeated by a morally and humanly superior one. I knew it wasn't a matter of pro-life dogma for him, either churchy or political. It was part of his love for Anna, and for the fruit of that love now growing in her body. "I'm just trying to make sure that you have your eyes open about this," I said. "This may be the biggest decision you'll ever make in your life."

His tone softened and his voice lowered. "Dad, I know you're trying to look out for me and I appreciate that, but there's no way that we're killing this baby. No way. I really have a feeling that this is the right thing. This baby is going to be something totally special and I'm going to protect it no matter what."

Though at that point I didn't yet know about Elaine's supportive reaction, I found myself thinking something similar. Maybe it would energize him and inspire a new chapter of his life. He would be drawn into the orbit of something larger than himself. His subsequent behavior seemed to confirm that view. He drove to Anna's parents' home the next day and told them how things were, said he was prepared to take full responsibility for everything, and insisted that he and Anna were completely resolved about their decision. It was not an easy conversation, but when Oliver stood firm, the family gave their blessing. Even today, in the light of all that has happened, I can't help feeling that it was one of his finest moments.

The long list of his adversities chronicles
the decade-long war between the deep strength
of heart that animated his best intentions and
the truly maniacal demon of his addiction. It
extended beyond any one drug or even any one
category of drugs. His craving for nicotine, the first
of his addictions, already seemed unusually intense.
He rarely seemed to really enjoy smoking—
this said by someone who smoked with great
pleasure on and off for years. It seemed more like
gratifying a gnawing need. Unknown to us at the
time, he went through a full gamut of substances
on his way to heroin—marijuana, LSD, ecstasy,
cocaine, Oxycontin—consuming great quantities
of each. He regularly imbibed a range of
prescription pills, pretty much anything he could
get his hands on.

He also drank alcohol with a voraciousness
that amazed me, often in combination with other
drugs. He went through an especially big "Bud
Ice" period during which he favored the twenty-
four-ounce bottles with the blue aluminum screw
cap. Cleaning out his basement room after the
year that he lived with Becky and me, one of his
better years, I found a sort of necklace made from
those blue caps, each one crushed flat like a coin,

holed, and strung on a piece of twine. It was eight feet long.

The path to his addiction that began with reckless behavior—flirtations with pot smoking and occasional drinking—quickly delivered him into the claws of a beast that utterly controlled him. As he sunk deeper, he came more and more to hate that beast. Yet he would furiously defend and protect it, most of all by conspiring to keep it hidden. Oliver employed every bit of his considerable intelligence and the full force of his personal charm to conceal his addiction and to deny its power over him. Looking back on it, that work of concealment, so expertly carried out, seems among the most decisive factors in his destruction, as it prevented us from intervening earlier, when we had the best chance of helping him. By the time we woke up to the reality of his situation, toward the end of his junior year in high school, he had been spiraling into the vortex of substance abuse for almost four years.

The later years of his addiction were agony for everyone connected to him. For anyone with no firsthand experience of it, the suffering imposed upon the loved ones of a drug addict is unimaginable. There are the ceaseless arguments and fights, accusations and counteraccusations, the long nights of worry, the broken windows and doors, the lying and thefts, the financial drain stemming from a seemingly endless variety of expenses. Then there are the run-ins with police and the wrangling with insurance companies, all in addition to the overdoses, accidents, beatings, hospitalizations, and suicide attempts.

The most debilitating damage is finally internal, a result of the barrier that inevitably comes to separate the drug user from others around him, a barrier of mutual distrust and suspicion, built over time, incident by injuring incident. For parents and loved ones of addicts, the hardest task is separating love and concern from enabling the addiction. The toughest thing about tough love is knowing when and how to use it. Loaning them money is obviously out. But what about the time that I bought Oliver a leaf blower to help launch his fledgling gutter-cleaning business? It sounded like a good idea at the time. But then again, he blew most of the profits on drugs. Was it really helping, then?

One commonly hears it said about addicts that their need for the drug becomes more important than their need for love, that the drug actually replaces love and makes it irrelevant. My own experience tells me that's too simple. The truth is not only more complicated but also more excruciating. Until the very end, love still lives and breathes at the heart of every addiction, but does so in a vicious cycle of deepening degradation. With each descent into drug use, the addict violates the hopes and cares of those closest to them and then pays for those injuries with an ever-intensifying sense of failure. Whatever the neurochemical roots of an addict's cravings, the next fix is also required to blunt a deepening self-hatred. In this way, addiction feeds on the energy of love in a distorted and malignant cycle, the way a cancerous tumor siphons off the body's growth-producing blood for its own enlargement.

It is this self-devouring entanglement of love at the core of the addictive process that makes getting away from the immediate family for a significant stretch of time a nearly indispensable condition of recovery. The noxious cycle of love, violation, and self-contempt has to be interrupted before the drug-addicted person can repossess their own powers of regeneration. To be freed from that terrible circuit, what's needed is an extended period of isolation from loved ones, as if they themselves are a major source of the problem. The blood supply to the tumor has to be cut off.

Of course, another way out is suicide. The four-page record of Oliver's torments amply shows why addicts so often kill themselves. But suicide is an exit only for the one who commits it. For those left behind, the agony goes on. Authors of books about death and mourning list factors that increase the difficulty of grieving: the unexpectedness of the death, the degree of violence involved, the youth of the deceased, and so on. Oliver's death rang the bell in every category.

When I get to Elaine's in the afternoon, Anna has just arrived with Jack. This is to be the moment that she tells him that his father is dead and that he won't be coming back. Until now, she had tried to satisfy his curiosity and apprehension with the story that his Daddy got very sick, that he had to go to the hospital, and that he couldn't come home right now. There is still quite a crowd at the apartment and everyone feels the tension of the approaching moment. It is a warm afternoon and when the time comes, Anna takes Jack out into the backyard, a spacious expanse of grass and trees, uncommonly large for such a relatively small apartment. They sit together for fifteen or twenty minutes. Inside, all of us are painfully aware of what is transpiring in the backyard. Very little is said. Except for the constant smoking—apparently for others, too, the preferred response to Oliver's death—we might be a circle of schoolchildren squirming outside the principal's office, painfully aware of what's happening to the kid who just got taken behind the door.

Just a few minutes before Anna comes back inside, a phone call comes in from Elaine's mother and, not long after Jack has reentered the house, he is summoned to the phone to speak with his great-grandmother. It was overhearing that phone call from the next room that gave us the first clue about how Anna had broken the news to him.

"Your Daddy got very, very sick, Jackson, and finally he died," Anna had begun.

"But will he come back to see me?" Jack asked.

"No, Jack. He was so sick that he died. When someone dies, they don't come back. Daddy died and he's in heaven now. He won't be coming back to see us."

Anna tried to reassure him that the other people in his life weren't going to die, that you had to be really, really sick to die and that didn't happen very often. But Jack immediately had other ideas.

"So, can I go see Daddy in heaven?"

"No," Anna said, "heaven's a place that's really far away. Daddy can't come here and we can't go to heaven."

"Where is heaven?" Jack then wanted to know.

"Heaven is somewhere way up high," Anna said, "like the clouds and the sky where the birds fly. We can't go where the birds fly, can we? Well, heaven's like that. We can't go to heaven."

As he picks up the phone in the kitchen, Jack's three-year-old voice is easily audible for all of us next door in the living room. After a minute or two, we hear him say, with an innocent matter-of-factness that seems violently out of keeping with the gravity of the moment, "Yeah, my daddy got really, really sick and he died." A pause follows in which he listens to whatever is said on the other end of the line. "Yes, that's right," he continues in the same matter-of-fact tone, "my daddy died and he's a bird now."

# *11*

The previous session with Barbara felt like a
revelation. The keynote was the pattern of putting
myself at a distance from people—of perching
myself in a treetop. It now seems like the secret
of my aesthetic sense, my intellectual style, my
passion for philosophy. It's the red thread running
through my whole personality.

But is that really right? Am I really at such a
distance from my family? If I'm honest about it,
I have to admit I'm often at the center of things,

the one everyone expects to host a holiday get-together, or to write a poem for a big birthday.

I'm confused. Was my big revelation just bogus? Maybe I'm not the rebel-recluse that I take myself to be. In fact, don't I have to admit that I'm pretty flatly conventional?

If we're talking about withdrawing from the family circle and declaring independence, my brother is much more up a tree and out to sea than I've ever been. Far from fulfilling my parents' hopes, he horrified them by dropping out of his first year of college and joining the Unification Church of Sun Myung Moon. Jim became a "Moonie" and remains in the church to this day. My father agonized over it. If one of us is really "out there," daring to go outside the family, it's Jim, not me.

For Jim, joining the church was a very real rebellion, a wholesale rejection of his family. And yet, ironically, the Moon church is nothing if not a cult of family, with the ultimate father figure at the top. If becoming a Moonie meant rejecting one father, it meant spectacularly embracing another.

Did I, too, arrive at some symptomatic solution, some way of serving both sides of a conflict, having it both ways? Of course! It was becoming a doctor. In my high school years, I was sure I wanted a career in medicine. But even then, I knew my aims were linked with my father's unmet ambitions. Being a doctor was my dream in large part because it was his. So I did become a doctor after all, just not a physician. As a Ph.D., I got some of the prestige of the title, but also took a distance from my father. My choice of philosophy could hardly have been more foreign to him.

"You really did have it both ways, pleasing your parents but doing it on your own terms."

Yes, both ways in the extreme. The subtler structure of my own neurotic compromise clarifies like a ship coming out of the fog.

On one side, there was the familiar image of myself, the happy boy, the sunny spirit of the family. I was the consummate pleaser, the one whose self-assigned business it was to make everybody feel good. I always recognized myself in the joke about the optimist and the pessimist as two kids on Christmas morning who find a giant load of horse manure under the tree. The pessimist immediately complains, "This is nothing but a pile of shit!" "You bet!" exclaims the optimist, "and with all this crap there's got to be a pony in here somewhere!"

But that happy-boy role was largely a mask, a fantasy constructed to conceal a good deal of internal sadness and loneliness. That inner pain had requirements of its own—it drove me to the treetop—but I wasn't willing to let any of it show. And what better way to hide being unhappy than merely to pretend I wasn't?

As if allaying the pain of feeling like I never really belonged, that despite all appearances I felt like an outsider to the family, a childhood memory pops into mind, that of my grandfather gently stroking the back of my neck. He did it often, distractedly, riding in the car or sitting around

the living room after dinner, watching the fire.
He would trace the skin just at the hairline with
his fingertips. It would deliver me into a blissful
trance. Yes, like a drug.

While this sweet image is still flickering in
my mind, another memory from Turner
unexpectedly erupts, as traumatic as the one
about my grandfather's touch was idyllic. It is
the memory of killing a giant snapping turtle,
the largest of several big turtles I caught in those
years. I was ten.

Bad enough to have killed him, but we also failed
in our plan to preserve his shell. I remember
thinking at the time that he was probably older
than any of us. In a strange and primitive way, he
was a superior being. And it was my fault that it
happened. It was only my desire to catch him that
did him in.

The worst was the act of killing it. It happened on
the beach. My father allowed my brother and me
to shoot it with the .22 rifle. When the first bullet
struck it in the head, it tore away a great chunk of

flesh. The interior tissue was strangely, alarmingly white, immediately trellised with fine lines of crimson as the blood began to flow. The pale flesh traced with red contrasted monstrously with the dark green crust of his ancient shell.

But the truly uncanny and terrifying thing was that, once shot, his head ripped open horribly, the turtle didn't die. The force knocked his head to the ground, but then it rose up again. He recovered and continued to move, pawing the wet sand with his claws, turning his wounded head from side to side. Yet another bullet, and five or six more after that, also failed to kill him. He just kept looking around, his head more and more terribly mangled, as if he were merely befuddled by all the commotion.

The walls of the room close in on me. My chest constricts and I struggle to get my breath.

*It's the dream of shooting myself.*

Just like the memory of the turtle, the dream was dominated by a horrific awareness of the damage done by a bullet, damage that could not be undone. And I, too, had astonishingly failed to die.

Another shock follows immediately with the thought of that last bullet, the one that killed my son. Three bullets, three heads blown open, three moments of excruciating regret. My ears ring. I fear I'm going to pass out.

It seems like a dark cipher over the whole trajectory of my life. In three terrible moments, a bullet irretrievably destroys something of priceless value. Three experiences of desperately wishing that time could be rolled back to undo some fatal damage. I cannot help feeling that it was, three times over, the same bullet.

I feel compelled to tell Barbara the whole story.

It was a clear, calm morning, the sun just rising over the hill on the far side of the lake. I was going out fishing with my father, a somewhat unusual event in those days, as I had become so well accustomed to going alone. The glassy surface allowed a perfect vision of the bottom even in ten feet of water. It was at about that depth that I recognized the dark oval of a great turtle's shell.

There he was. Close on the bottom, the cone of his snout just poking out from under the edge of his enormous shell. I naturally thought of catching him, but he was much too deep for the net. Then I had an idea—a long shot, for sure. I rigged a three-pronged spoon and lowered it slowly toward him. Then it suddenly seemed easy. The hook caught under the front edge of the shell and held fast. We began very slowly paddling toward shore. Surely, I thought, he'll make a break for it at any moment. But he didn't. He lay like a sleeping baby on the end of the line.

When we reached the shallows, he seemed suddenly to awaken. I thrust the fishing pole at my father and jumped out of the boat, thinking to use my paddle as a prod. Just as I got to him, the line broke. My father, too, jumped into the knee-deep water and between the two of us we heaved him to shore, his powerful claws motoring for all he was worth. He emerged just short of the beach, hissing and blowing. After a few moments, he stopped struggling. He eyed us, as if sizing up the situation, as if he wasn't sure what his next step might be.

We managed, straining with both paddles, to spoon him into the canoe, then walked the boat back to the cottage along the long, narrow strand of beach.

Over breakfast the idea surfaced—it was my father's—that we ought to take his shell. I was immediately enchanted. What a trophy it would make mounted on the living room wall! Something of my own to compare with my father's magnificent five-pound bass.

Also a suggestion of my father's was the plan to separate the shell from the turtle's flesh by boiling him in one of the old washtubs from the garage. Just like cooking chicken meat off the bones, he said. My brother and I set it up on the outdoor fireplace where we burned the trash. But the whole thing went pathetically awry when the shell disintegrated along with everything else. After working at it for most of the morning, we ended up having to bury the miserable remains of the turtle at the bottom of the washtub, now a black, sad, lumpy mass.

In beginning my analysis, I wondered if there would be a moment of crisis, of finding some deep kernel of truth and confronting it. I even feared I might never get to it. But now that it's here, welling up in me with gut-twisting force, I'm completely unprepared. I struggle to compose myself to speak.

I feel like that turtle. I feel like something shot in the head but not dead.

There's a long, tense pause, then a near whisper, as if from very far away.

"Animals can mean a great deal to us."

Her simple words are wrenching and the tears flood.

Recalling it over forty years later, I'm astonished by the freshness of the memory. I suppose that's what Freud meant by the timelessness of the

unconscious—the trace of trauma preserved
in memory like an ancient mummy whose eyes
might pop open at any moment and glisten, bright
and wet. It is as though that turtle is still on that
beach, stunned from the first bullet fired into its
head, still struggling to know which way he might
turn to reach the safety of the water. I still feel
deeply guilty about it.

My cheeks wash over with sadness and regret. It
is as if I, the one who fired the first two of those
bullets—the one on the beach and the one in the
dream—also fired the third one, the bullet that
killed my son.

But it's strange—it comes to me in an odd pause—
I can't remember whether I actually fired the
gun that morning. It makes sense that it was
my brother who did it. He was the violent one,
the bully, the one who would beat me up for the
hell of it. My withdrawal to my own world, up
my tree or out on the lake, was in the main an
escape from him, a refusal of everything that he
represented.

But did I, too, fire that gun?

The half-admission in the question brings the crucial realization. The whole, terrible episode sparked a dreadful short circuit between my brother and myself. By my own act, the distance that I had constructed between us collapsed. I had become him.

It finally makes perfect sense. I was guilty of the very thing that I most hated about my brother— his tireless, aggressive self-promotion. That turtle would have been a badge of my own achievement, a sort of treasure brought back from the lake that I had claimed as my lonely dominion.

Of course I couldn't remember whether I fired the gun or not. Any such act of violence, especially violence in the service of pride and ambition, was the very thing that I couldn't tolerate in myself. Wasn't that the core of the happy-boy fantasy?

Don't I have to admit it? The good-boy mask was more than a cover for an inner sadness, it also concealed an underlying rage. The mask was a fantasy built on the contrast between my brother and myself, a rejection of everything associated

with him. The escape into my private world
served to preserve that contrast. It rehearsed that
rejection but also hid it from me. A potent streak
of rage remained despite my own denial.

A scene from *Lawrence of Arabia* flashes into mind.
Lawrence has returned from his triumph in
capturing the port city of Aqaba. Still dressed in
his filthy Arab robes, he's sitting in the grand hall
of Allenby's headquarters in Cairo, answering
the general's questions about "what happened
out there." The magnitude of his achievement is
remarked by Dryden, Allenby's political advisor.
"Before he did it, sir," Dryden says, "I'd have said
it couldn't be done." Couldn't the same be said—
at least in the mind of a ten-year-old kid—for
capturing that enormous turtle? Before I did it,
who would have believed it could be done?

But it's more than that. On the long march to
Aqaba, Lawrence rescues one of the Bedouin
recruits, Gassim, who had been lost in the desert.
Lawrence brings him back from the sand-sea,
a trophy of his own skill and endurance. Later,
when Gassim kills a member of another tribe in a

petty dispute, it falls to Lawrence to execute him. Standing over him at point-blank range, he shoots him in the head.

When he confesses it to Allenby, Lawrence adds: "There was something about it that I didn't like." No shame in the killing required by war, Allenby tries to say. But Lawrence persists: "No, something else." Allenby pushes back: "What then?" And Lawrence answers, spitting it out like venom: "I enjoyed it."

The thoughts are coming faster than I can keep up with them. The pistol that Lawrence used to execute Gassim is precisely the pistol in my dream of shooting myself. That pistol is a central element of the film, reappearing several times and forming a crucial unifying thread of the story. Early on, Lawrence gives it to his Arab guide as a token of trust. In the next scene, the guide is himself shot to death by a bullet in the head.

Is there no bottom to this well of correspondences? I feel like I can't take any more. I want to blink and find myself elsewhere, anywhere. But once the consistency of the fantasy has been ruptured, the consequences unfold by themselves.

My whole self-image—it's excruciating to admit it—has functioned to hide the force of my own anger. I remember early childhood scenes of my rage in full blossom. Taunted by my brother, I would flail at him in a white heat of rage that I was completely impotent to satisfy.

It explains the plague dream, the plague that would eventually kill everyone. It's the ultimate dream of revenge. The hyperrational coolness with which I shot myself is perfect, too. It's all of a piece with my general strategy of dealing with anger. I draw off to a safe distance.

"Like you're keeping everybody safe?"

Yes! The truth is that I've always had a hard time expressing anger, or even fully feeling it. It's often struck me on the tennis court. Guys I play with can be angered by their own mistakes, but are then able to put that anger to work in playing better. Not me. The madder I get, the tighter and more prone to errors I become. It's a vicious circle of accelerating but impotent rage. I've often told myself that I'm just not that competitive. What crap. The problem isn't being insufficiently competitive but precisely the opposite. I'm competitive to the point of wanting blood.

The light of this perspective on my marriage to Elaine is especially harsh. To all appearances, our union was almost seamlessly loving and placid. We very rarely fought openly, and when we did, I was quick to assume the fault. Among our friends, our marriage seemed like a sort of ideal. But it was a sham harmony. The fact was that I couldn't tolerate my own anger at her, an anger that I had ample means of denying, or—much more importantly—of expressing in other, more quietly destructive ways. What was a love affair but just another tree house?

I had always told myself that Elaine was the problem in our marriage. There was her sullen disapproval of my decision to pursue a career as an academic. And also her general tendency to withdraw from energy or exertion or excitement, her predictable resistance to social situations,

to loud music, to going to a play or a lecture,
to hosting people for dinner. It all spawned an
anger in me that I hid from myself, an anger that
I acted out without any real awareness of what
motivated me.

How, then, might it have affected Oliver? I
feel compelled to draw the full measure of
self-accusation.

I know that he found the bond between his mother
and me hard to understand. On an evening walk
together when he was perhaps fourteen years
old, he asked me about what glued us together.
"You guys have nothing in common," he said, not
without a painful measure of truth. "I don't get it,
Dad," he said, "why are you together at all?"

I remember falling back on our long history
together (which just begged the question). And I
think I said something about opposites attracting
(hardly a satisfying answer). But I knew, even at
the time, that he was struggling to make sense of
his own family. Yet how could he? Even now, I
have a hard time understanding it myself.

This line of questioning presses on my mind like an unwelcome intruder. If I find my own anger hard to bear, if I hide it even from myself, it's striking that Oliver had nothing like the same problem. Over the last years of his life he became increasingly quick-tempered, and by the end he was prone to rages that were truly terrifying. Surely he didn't feel the least constrained by the need to maintain any image of good-boy sunniness. Was it just the terrible grip of the addiction that bent him in the direction of all that rage? Or is it possible that he assumed the very current of anger that I myself disavowed?

Surely it's the last thing that I would have expected. During the final few years of his life, I found Oliver's proneness to anger completely foreign, and really terrifying. I sometimes wondered how he could be related to me at all. But was I seeing in my son, as in an inverting mirror, a force of rage that I couldn't tolerate in myself?

Trying to get some grip on myself, yet also grateful for the opportunity to cry it out some more, I tell Barbara that I feel like apologizing.

I lie on the couch for several long minutes and bawl like a baby. Then it passes, like a summer storm. A strange relaxation comes over me, more surprising even than the winding train of reflections that had preceded it. It feels, I say, like having vomited something up.

It feels—I can barely choke out the words—like I've had a bullet removed.

# *12*

Anna amazes me with her resilience. Somewhere, beneath her reassuring appearance of courage and stability, I know that she must be deeply injured and exhausted by the whole, terrible tragedy.

By Friday morning we've found a new apartment for her that seems adequate for her needs and within her spare budget. We buy a new bed that will be delivered later in the day. It remains to collect a larger load of stuff from the old place. Oliver's best friend Whit wants to help and just after noontime the three of us meet at the door. The horrid yellow police tape still hangs limply from the frame. No one has been in the apartment since I left it three days ago.

Whit has come home from Frostburg State for the funeral. In years past, he and Oliver were inseparable, though over the last year or two their friendship, like virtually all of Oliver's relationships, became a casualty of his addiction. Now, sitting in the apartment where Oliver shot himself to death, Whit seems stunned by it all, unable to believe that his friend is gone and that he exited the world so violently. Though Whit is a good deal more familiar with firearms than me, he, too, found Oliver's fascination with guns ominous. And while he is no stranger to drugs, the raging ferocity of Oliver's addiction is alien to him. When he sees the bloodstained mattress, the cold reality of what has happened hits him and he bursts into tears. The three of us take refuge in the living room and stand there in a long, tearful, three-way embrace.

"I just can't believe that he would do it," Whit says, flopping into the big armchair that Oliver preferred on the many nights he drank himself to sleep. Hearing him say it brings the contradiction back to me as well. The stark reality of Oliver's suicide seems impossible to reconcile with the ebullient, sensitive, good-humored spirit whom we all loved so much.

"There were a lot of things that Oliver didn't tell anyone," Anna says, "not even me. I loved him so much. He was like no one else I've ever met. So caring, and so perceptive about things. He would notice things about people that no one else would pick up on and he could be so thoughtful. When things were good, they were really great. But there were lots of times that I felt like he wouldn't let me in, like there was some part of him that he wouldn't let me see. The weird thing is, we would have talks sometimes and he would be so great, so completely there, and I would think, okay, he gets it, we're going to get through this. But then the next day, it would be like we never talked at all. He would just shut down and become someone else."

Her description is excruciatingly familiar to me. I, too, had wonderful moments of feeling connected with him. I thought of the time, nine months earlier, when he asked me to come shooting with him. He took enormous pride in showing me how to load and aim the guns, two pistols and a shotgun for skeet. He had invited me into his element, a world apart from everything else. As long as we lingered there, we seemed to enjoy an easy and immensely welcome camaraderie. But leaving that sphere was like a door closing. The open avenue of access to him was suddenly shut. It was as if being armed had become for him the indispensable condition of any intimacy at all.

"He really changed, Whit," Anna says. "He wasn't the same Oliver you knew. These last months, he was really crazy. He thought people were after him all the time. He would stay up at night and look out the windows because he thought that cops were in the parking lot watching the house. He ripped the covers off the heating vents because he was convinced that somebody had put bugs in there for listening to him. One night he went out to the parking lot and accused some guy of spying on us. The guy was freaked out, and then he got really pissed. They almost got into a fight. It was so scary. I didn't know what was going to happen."

I had been aware of Oliver's growing paranoia, though it horrifies me to hear Anna describe some of his more bizarre behavior. Even with all that's happened, I hadn't taken seriously enough the possibility that he was descending into real madness. Is it because his final decline had happened so fast? Or was I just in denial, not wanting to believe it?

I think again about the guns and about his terrifying comment just a month earlier about "going down to the mall." My phone calls to the police and to his psychiatrist were what triggered his last and most dramatic outburst of anger at me. I had even begun to fear for Anna and Jack. The responses of psychiatrists I talked to were equivocal at best. They said it was almost impossible to correctly diagnose someone in such active addiction. "Dual diagnosis," they called it. The symptoms of many serious psychiatric disorders are mimicked by the cycles of drug use and withdrawal. Bipolar disorder, among other things famously associated with proclivities toward suicide, certainly fit the bill and was more than once mentioned to us as a likely possibility. But in the midst of his struggle with drugs there was no way to know with any certainty.

We continue to talk for a while, briefly reminiscing about times past, when Oliver was his old, wonderful self. "I loved that guy," says

Whit. "He would get us to do stuff that nobody else even thought of doing. He had the best sense of adventure."

"Like your escapades at Prettyboy Reservoir," I say.

"Yeah, Oliver loved those times. We'd be at some party somewhere and out of the blue he'd say, 'It's Prettyboy time,' and we'd take off right then, in the middle of the night. He knew the trails up there so well we'd make it down to the water in the dark. We'd build a fire and stay all night. He liked that better than anything."

But eventually we all fall silent. The unrelenting finality of his death chokes every impulse to say more. It is a relief to lose ourselves in the mindless labor of loading some furniture into the back of Whit's truck. When we're done, he and Anna leave. I will stay and await the arrival of the man I've hired to drill open Oliver's gun safe, the combination to which only he had known.

Alone in the apartment, I again go into the bedroom and sit down on the mattress, feeling numb and blank. Then it occurs to me—crazy that I didn't think of it before—I'll need to take the whole thing out of the room. The poor fellow who has to open the safe shouldn't have to step over the bloody remains of my son's suicide. Yet I wince at the idea of getting rid of it. The bloodstained mattress cover feels like the last shred of physical connection with him. I don't want to let it go. Sick at heart, I force myself to cut the cover off and cram it into one of the plastic bags containing the rest of the soiled bedclothes. I can't resist saving a little piece of the blood-marked fabric, which I stuff in the back pocket of my jeans. I then haul the bags and finally the mattress itself out to the dumpster.

Not long after, the safe man arrives. He's a young guy, a little heavy-set, with a red stubble of beard that immediately reminds me of Oliver. He never asks what happened, and I don't offer to tell him. He simply sets about his task, which turns out to be surprisingly easy. So easy, in fact, that the safe is drilled open before I am ready for it. I have been intensely curious to know what is inside but now realize that I am also anxious about it.

When the big door swings open, I'm disappointed that the safe is mostly empty. I had hoped it might contain some clue about the meaning of his death, some note left behind, maybe a journal of his writings. Anything that would answer some of the agonizing questions that still weigh heavily on me.

The safe contains three guns, along with some ammunition and a pistol holster. Especially disturbing is the semiautomatic rifle, the same one that lay behind him on the couch the day I came to the apartment two months earlier. Fully loaded, with a second magazine clip taped commando-style to the gun stock, it makes me shudder to remember his comment about a shooting spree at the mall. The safe man, himself a skilled gun enthusiast, deftly unloads the thing, detaching the clip from the base of the gun with a single, easy motion and checking the firing chamber to make sure it is empty. He does the same with the two pistols. They, too, are fully loaded.

When the fellow leaves, the silence of the apartment enfolds me. I seize on the only other things that remain in the safe: three pieces of paper, each placed neatly on the top shelf. One is the obituary notice for Oliver's friend Jim, who died of a heroin overdose a year earlier. I knew how hard it hit Oliver at the time and I wonder how it might have played as a sort of prelude to his suicide.

There is also a delicate scrap of unusually textured paper with a black woodblock print on it. The crude print shows waves on a body of water beneath the rising moon. I recognize it as a memento from his trip to Nepal and Tibet, a trip that we had arranged for him when he turned sixteen. At the time, Elaine and I were still not fully aware of his developing drug dependency, but we knew that his sophomore year had been difficult. He had quit the lacrosse team and had all but stopped playing his bass guitar. My own transformative experience of travel abroad made me hopeful that he might experience something similar. The program was called "Where There Be Dragons." In fact, he passed his sixteenth birthday while trekking on the Tibetan plateau. I have a photograph of him, beaming with happiness before a candle-bedecked cake—as credible a birthday cake as one might manage to bake in the middle of nowhere—surrounded by a dozen or more young people, a mix of Westerners and Tibetans. He especially loved the week of home stay with a family in rural Nepal. I have a picture of that time, too. It sits on one of the file cabinets in my office at the college. There he is, surrounded by a little throng of kids, most of them looking at him with wide-eyed grins, while Oliver himself is looking out at the camera with the most shining smile I ever saw on him.

The only other object in the safe is a birthday card from me. It was laid carefully on the top shelf between the obituary notice and the print. The cover is an image of Southwestern canyon rocks, the undulating red sandstone that we both fell in love with in Colorado. I had sent it to him a year and a half earlier, on his twenty-second birthday, when he was already deep into his addiction to heroin.

*July 23, 2004*

*Dear Oliver,*

*Twenty-two years—I can't believe it's passed so fast! I remember it like it was yesterday, driving over the Charles River Bridge on the way to the hospital when you were born. A thunderstorm had just blown through and there was a double rainbow in the east and a really breathtaking sunset in the west. It's been a lot of adventures since then! Like running up the down escalators in Boston with*

*Deb, catching turtles and burning campfires at*
*Turner with me. And our great trip to Colorado.*
*Then playing soccer in Baltimore, trekking in*
*Nepal, and a thousand other places in between. I*
*wish for you a long life of further adventures, in*
*which you recover and relive the things you've done,*
*and also discover and live with joy and wonder a*
*host of new things.*

*In the end, it is the people that we've known*
*and loved who stay with us—it is they who give*
*the places meaning—and I will always have you*
*in my heart and remember the places we've been*
*together.*

> *Happy Birthday Oliver.*
> *With much love,*
>
> > *Dad*

I return to the living room and sit for a long time, thinking about his addiction. How much was it, as clinicians sometimes say, a matter of genetic predisposition? The ferocity of his cravings, along with the range and quantities of drugs he consumed, make an organic explanation seem tempting. Surely there were psychological factors as well, particularly anxiety. I'd often thought that a great share of his need for drugs was an effort to self-medicate. During his first year in high school, he had classic anxiety attacks in the hallway between classes, the kind that dizzyingly constricts one's vision, as if looking at the world through a blackened pipe. As we later learned, it was around that time that he started smoking weed before school with a little band of buddies. It was like trying to put out a fire by dousing it with gasoline.

What torments me most are my fears of the part played by his relation to me. How badly had I failed him? I know that he felt bitterly betrayed and deeply angry at me. There was the recent episode of my calling his psychiatrist, the episode that prompted the savage phone message he left for me.

Of course, there was also his discovery of my love affair that led to my separation from his mother. After I left, I tried desperately to get us into family counseling together, if only to clear the air between the three of us. But both Elaine and Oliver refused to return after our first and only session. I don't know how he had felt about my later becoming involved with Rebecca and finally remarrying, but it's easy to suspect the worst. During the year that he lived with us, relations between him and Rebecca were always somewhat strained.

The most wrenching episode of all was when we had him involuntarily put into treatment at a special recovery center in Baja, Mexico. Two daughters of a colleague of mine at the college had been saved by the program there, and it came highly recommended by a circle of other people I interviewed by phone. We made the hard decision to have him taken there just two months after I moved out of the house. It was the fall of his senior year in high school and we knew that once he turned eighteen, placing him in treatment against his will would be impossible. It seemed like the last chance we had to free him from the addiction that was eating him alive.

Elaine couldn't bear to be present when the two-person team came for him, and he clearly regarded the whole plan as my doing. The most devastating moment came only ten or twelve hours after they left Baltimore. His caretakers called from San Diego to say that Oliver had escaped, ducking out the men's room window at a Denny's restaurant. They said that nobody had ever gotten away from them before. You don't know my son, I told them. For a brief moment, even amid my panic and intense frustration, I was almost pleased by it. It was a perfect emblem of Oliver's fierce independence and resourcefulness. Reckless and self-destructive though it was, it was also an act of courage, carried out at considerable risk to himself.

The real crisis came later that night, when he and I finally connected by phone and I got him to check into a motel. He agreed only on condition that I not tell the Teen Care Camp people where he was. He wanted me to fly out and bring him home. Hanging up the phone, immensely relieved that he was safe for the moment, the enormity of my dilemma began to sink in. I could keep my promise to him and bring him home, or I could break it and follow through with our plan to put him into treatment, even against his will. I stayed up long into the night with Elaine and an old mutual friend, agonizing over what course of action would be best. Elaine was indecisive and Eric was reluctant to tell me what to do. I spent hours on the phone with parents of kids who had been through the program and who were eager to vouch for its successes.

I finally resolved, in a mix of agony and exhaustion, that I would break my promise. It was without any doubt the most wrenching decision I've ever made. I knew very well that if he ever forgave me for it, it would be only years later, maybe realizing that, however painful and scary, it was the right thing for him. It felt like cutting my own arm off.

The end of the Teen Care Camp episode was singularly bizarre and confusing. During our first visit to the program, just two weeks into his stay, Oliver seemed terrible. He was sullen, angry, and distant. We left feeling sick with fear that we'd made a horrible mistake. But on our next visit, only five weeks later, the change in him was astonishing. He was radiant. He had made a circle of friends and was drawing and reading again. His room was filled with beautiful rocks and pieces of driftwood that he had found on the beaches of Baja. His speech was clear, strong, and direct, his eyes bright and shining. I was overjoyed at the transformation and felt, for one glorious moment, that we had our son back, the Oliver I loved so dearly.

But then, on the second day of our visit, disaster. During our time alone with him, he told us that he had been molested by the camp director. My jaw dropped in horror and disbelief, less at the charge itself than by the contradiction that it seemed to imply. How to reconcile this claim of abuse with the miraculously beaming and happy boy who stood in front of me? Yet Oliver's friend, Chris, seemed to confirm the story, claiming to have heard a rumor of it from others.

Was it true, then? Neither Elaine nor Chris's parents, who were also visiting, were in any mood to doubt it. They all insisted that we leave the place at once, without even confronting the director about Oliver's accusation. In agony over the prospect of making him feel that I was betraying him yet again by refusing to believe what he was telling us, I relented and we left in the time it took to gather the boys' things. I figured that we would sort out the rest when we got back to San Diego.

We never learned what really happened. Oliver refused to talk about it. It's quite possible he was telling the truth, possible even that whatever may have happened between him and the director wasn't bad enough to undo the good effects of seven drug-free weeks in a beautiful place. It's also possible that he very skillfully manipulated the whole situation toward the end of getting himself home. He was certainly capable of such things. Which is right? I will never know.

Sitting in the silence of his apartment, recalling that terrible episode, I'm overtaken by the uncertainty that seems to engulf everything about his life and death. It descends on me like an enormous, suffocating weight. The whole nightmare of the past ten years rises up before me as a monstrous enigma. I don't know the causes of his addiction. I don't know why he so adamantly refused treatment. I don't know whether, or to what extent, he might have been suffering all along from an increasingly debilitating mental illness. I don't know why he killed himself.

# 13

"Daphne, you look fabulous, you're positively glowing!" The words are out of my mouth before I realize that even for one of Rebecca's colleagues in the orchestra, someone I know fairly well, my choice for greeting her at the stage door might sound a bit forward.

She laughs, pauses a second, and says, "Yes, actually, I am pretty fabulous! I just had the most interesting experience." Then pausing again, as if deciding whether to share her beauty secret, she exclaims, "But the perfect person for this is you! *You* would love this."

The "this" in question was participating in a special research study at Johns Hopkins Hospital in which volunteers are given a hefty dose of psilocybin, the psychoactive substance in "magic mushrooms." "It made me feel like a new person," Daphne says, beaming more than ever. She knew about my philosophical bent and had good reason to think that I would find a psychedelic experience attractive, if only for the promise of delivering a wildly altered state of consciousness.

Despite coming of age with the hippie generation, and despite having smoked my share of marijuana, I had never dropped acid nor risked any other hallucinogenic drug. I was tempted more than once, but always chickened out. Somewhere in the back of my mind, I would replay the dire rumors about bad trips, uncontrolled flashbacks, even genetic mutations, that circulated so feverishly in the early seventies. Yet I also nursed a lingering curiosity, and now, faced with the possibility of experiencing a major psychedelic in a safe environment, I felt tempted again. On a lark, I called the Hopkins number Daphne gave me. To my surprise, I was instantly granted a place in the study and invited to come for an initial interview.

That was only a couple of months before Oliver's final crisis. In the wake of his death, however, the prospect of launching myself into a state of hallucinogenic psychosis seemed out of the question. I felt like I was already in one. It was not until the better part of a year later, well into the course of my analysis, that the idea came back. It seemed like exactly what I needed. After many months on Barbara's couch, I was impatient with the analytic process and was hungry for some different kind of exploring. I wanted to push myself, and to be pushed. Even at the price of a potentially harrowing experience, I wanted to get to the bottom of my soul.

I called Mary Cosimano, the staff person who had interviewed me almost a year earlier. To my amazement, there was still an open slot in the study. But it was a new protocol. Not just a single active dose, as Daphne had, but five separate sessions spread over some months—four active doses and one placebo. I was also intrigued that the new study was focused specifically on the spiritual effects of psilocybin, a substance long used by many native peoples in rituals of spiritual exploration and transformation.

The aim of this latest study, directed by Roland Griffiths, a specialist in the psychological effects of various chemicals like nicotine and caffeine, was to answer a simple but fascinating question: is it possible that ingesting a particular substance can trigger a religious experience, or at least alter one's attitude toward religious belief? And how much more strange and thought-provoking that the substance in question this time was the natural product of a relatively common fungus.

It's a question that is taken up quite masterfully by Michael Pollan's recent book *How to Change Your Mind: What the New Science of Psychedelics Teaches Us About Consciousness, Dying, Addiction, Depression, and Transcendence.* Roland Griffiths is a key figure in the book. Pollan even interviewed me as one of the participants in the study and included some sections of the reports I wrote about my own experience with psilocybin.

Of course, the tantalizing prospect of participating in the study was greatly intensified by my desire to do something Oliver had done, to experience for myself the effects of some very powerful drug. I had already confessed to Rebecca that I was half-tempted to try heroin, if only to see what it was that Oliver had experienced. Some obscure part of me wanted to know firsthand what he had been through. "Are you nuts?" she immediately protested. "That's the craziest idea you've ever come up with. You're NOT doing that!"

My first visits to the Behavioral Sciences Building at Hopkins Bayview Hospital were anything but psychedelic, as they consisted largely of filling out whole stacks of questionnaires. There was one about my drug history (made easy by confessing my relative innocence) and several about my spiritual beliefs (in which I admitted to having been hot and cold about religion at different times in my life, but that I now felt like an agnostic, leaning toward atheism).

More interesting were the series of interviews with Mary and her colleague Matt Johnson, who would be caretaker "guides" for each of my sessions with the drug. We met in the room where I would spend those sessions—each one would take six hours or more—a room that looked and felt more like a comfortably appointed TV den than any hospital space I'd ever seen. They asked gentle but probing questions about my personal history from childhood to the present, prompted in part by looking through a little album of photos they had asked me to bring. The sense of personal connection established in those initial contacts was hugely important for my experience. As I was soon to learn, the effects of the drug are very powerfully shaped by one's expectations and by the feeling of comfort and safety one feels while under the drug's influence. "Set and setting," as they call it.

Oliver's life and death were of course a big part of those preliminary discussions. I immediately teared up when I showed them pictures of Oliver, one from his childhood and one taken on his twenty-second birthday. I was surprised but pleased that Mary and Matt didn't seem to think that my enduring torment of grief would pose any problem for the whole process.

When the time came for my first session, they encouraged me to be receptive to whatever happens, whatever appears. "You might think of it like being an astronaut going into outer space," Mary said. "Be open to seeing and feeling whatever happens. No two people experience the

drug in exactly the same way, and it's important
to know that there may be painful periods of
disorientation or anxiety. You may have some
really frightening moments. The best way to deal
with it," she advised, "is not to resist. Give in to
whatever happens. If a scary apparition shows
itself, go right up to it, embrace it with open arms,
and it will very likely dissolve into something
completely different."

As part of the research protocol, all participants
in the study were asked to write detailed reports
after each of their experiences with the drug. What
follows is a somewhat shortened version of my
first-session report—the session in which, I later
learned, I received my highest dose.

*Notes on My First Session with Psilocybin,*
*December 1, 2006*

Within a half hour of settling onto the couch
after taking my first dose, I am already feeling
physically strange—heavy and sluggish, as
if sinking deeper and deeper into a warm,
dark body of water. My sense of time feels
oddly warped, slowed and more riveted to

the intensities of the present. The sense of disorientation is increased both by the snug eyeshades and by the wowing selections of classical music being played on the headphones.

There are disturbances of my visual field, as if I am looking into an impossibly gigantic cavern, the ceiling of which begins to flicker with lights and movements. These shimmerings steadily increase in intensity and move in sync with the music with dizzying effect. Enormous organic shapes emerge, pulsing and dancing. I feel as if I am suspended in a galaxy every part of which is alive.

I realize early on that the hallucinogenic effects of the drug respond immediately to changes in my own subjective attitude. If I tense up with anxiety, the whole scene uncomfortably constricts. Jittering traces of light flicker across the visual field at odd angles, leaving me edgy and anxious. But if I consciously remind myself to relax, to just flow with the experience, the space in which I find myself softens, then yawns breathtakingly open. Over and over again, I have the sense of an infinite expanse being multiplied by yet another infinity.

The sheer gorgeousness of the music keeps washing over me with truly astounding force, at times becoming almost unbearably intense. At one point, I am so overwhelmed by the emotional tsunami of sound that I have to pull off the headset and take a break. Only slightly more stable in that moment, blinking in the suddenly bright light, I think to myself with a weirdly lucid sense of humor: "How strange that I'm still alive! Apparently one cannot die of too much beauty."

Midway into my trip, I feel a total loss of control. My entire sense of reality becomes completely unzipped. I can no longer tell where I am or what is happening to me. It is in many ways the most interesting part of the experience, though also the most terrifying. The trigger seems to be a weird reversal of cause and effect. Changes in the music, or Mary taking hold of my hand, seem to correspond immediately to my own desires, as if the fulfillment of my wishes occurs before I can even announce them to myself. The result is an insane mix of ecstasy and fear.

"Theories" of what is happening to me bubble up involuntarily. As I descend further and further into the maelstrom, some part of myself is apparently continuing to keep track of things, or at least attempting to. I think at one point, for example, that I am going insane. I seem to hear

Mary and Matt talking and become convinced that they are standing over me, horrified at the psychosis into which I have sunk, wondering helplessly what to do about it.

There are extremely bizarre experiences of language. Words shatter and recombine with other words. The name "Barbara" (my sister's name but also that of my psychoanalyst) is interspliced with "embarrassed" and repeated with wondrous effects. Other words ring in my ears in strange, rhyming chains. The echoing words also have instant effects on the unfolding hallucinations.

Another, somewhat later "theory" is that I am not in the room at Bayview at all but still lying in bed beside Rebecca, perhaps dreaming. I then become very anxious and agitated because I can't seem to find her. I'm like Dorothy in Oz, dropped into some unknown and mysterious place with no idea how I got there and no idea how to get back.

It gets worse. I have the urge to urinate and wonder if this urge is itself a hallucination. I then begin to think that, if I were to pee right here, it wouldn't really matter because none of this exists anyway. I move my arms and seem to encounter no resistance, but then wonder: "Am I really moving my arms or am I just thinking that I'm moving my arms? And how would I know the difference?" At one point, having again taken time out from the music headset though still blinded by the eyeshades, I feel myself grab a sheet of paper from the coffee table and feel hugely grateful to have found a solid piece of reality, something that pushes back against me. But when I hear the paper crinkle in my hand, the sound somehow registers as supercharged, as louder and more hypervividly *real* than it should be. Instead of reassuring me, it strikes me as yet another proof that everything has become totally *unreal.*

I'm then seized by a new, even more terrifying theory: I've become a heroin addict. This, I thought, is what Oliver experienced! Somehow, lost in the fog of grieving, trying in some crazy way to be with him, I have sunk into addiction myself. Is this what the grief over his death has led me to? And how can I possibly get out? Yet once again in the midst of this anxiety I feel so overcome with pleasure that I can't mobilize myself to feel bad about it. I think to myself, "now I see what he was after—surely this is worth dying for. What else matters? What does anything matter?"

At the depths of this insanity, I become convinced that I may be dying of an overdose or, more bizarrely, that I am already dead. All points of secure attachment to reality have ruptured. Yet I still think, "If this is dying, then okay. How can I say no to *this*?"

In the last few hours, reality begins slowly, impossibly, to stitch itself back together. During a particularly soaring passage of choral music, I have the sense of a triumphant reawakening, as if a new day is dawning after a long and terrifying night. The growing light feels like the "grand finale" of Fourth of July fireworks. The exhilaration is extraordinarily intense. Through most of the session, I felt like I was sinking into the darkest depths of the ocean, but I am now miraculously ascending back into the warmth and dazzling shine of the surface.

In the aftermath of the psilocybin experience, my feelings were complicated but almost wholly positive. My prime feeling was one of gratitude. A big part of it was the music. The overwhelming thrill of the sound, as if the pulse of reality itself had become audible, made me feel like I was hearing music—really hearing it—for the first time in my life. But the other part was Oliver. The terrors of my passage through the delirium gave way to an intense feeling of solidarity with him, a new sympathy for his addiction to heroin, and a deep feeling of being thankful for the chance to share something with him, even momentarily to *be* him.

In a subsequent session, I would meet him in another way.

# 14

My hope was that the psilocybin experience
would somehow complement my work in analysis,
but when I first told Barbara about the plan it felt
vaguely like a breach of contract. Or at least she
seemed to take it that way. She clearly resisted
the whole idea and told me so, reminding me
about the way many patients try to flee from the
process by throwing themselves into some other
involvement. But at the start of the session today
she says nothing. She's apparently back to playing
the silent analyst. It's just as well. I'm strangely

reluctant to attempt a description of my wild experience with the drug.

But I have bigger things on my mind, anyway. Our last session had left me with another, painfully pressing question. I'm still stunned by the whole turtle thing, still reeling from it. It's almost comical. It's my Oedipal moment, the fantasy of myself as a murderer. Do I fit the Freudian mold so patently? At the bottom, it's about unacknowledged rage. I've always thought of myself as slow to anger. A gentle person. Is that just false?

With a little honesty, I can fill out the indictment pretty easily. I'm embarrassed to admit it, but I often respond to frustrations with a daydream image of firing a machine gun. There I am, teeth clenched, eyes in a squint, spitting lead! Or when I make a mistake—especially something physical, like pounding my thumb with a hammer—my immediate response is a millisecond of blind fury. I've more than once smashed near-at-hand things I afterward regretted. I've had to warn Rebecca not to sneak up behind me and surprise me because my reflex is to whirl around and strike out.

"I'm thinking of your dream of the black lake. When you first talked about the dream, you said that it felt like the blackness was inside you."

Barbara's comment catches me off guard and I have to think for a moment. Yes, I did say that. Her recalling it produces a distinctly mixed emotion. Part of me is pleased by the feeling of being listened to and cared for. But I also feel oddly pressured, even threatened by it.

I'm casting about for a response.

What most struck me about the black water was its opacity. Even upon awakening, that inky darkness seemed strange because what always fascinated me most about the lake at Turner was its crystal clarity. Fishing in the morning calm, I enjoyed the thrill of gazing at the lake bottom even more than the prospect of catching something. For years I dreamed of building a glass-bottomed boat or some other Nemo-like contraption in which I could go exploring the depths.

*The summer he was six years old we caught a baby snapping turtle, its shell maybe three inches long. We were swimming and there he was, bobbing on the surface. Oliver begged to take it back to Baltimore to keep as a pet and, against my better judgment, I relented. Its name, of course, would be "Snappy." We kept it over the winter, feeding it carefully on a diet of fish and bits of raw hamburger. The turtle ate better than we did. The following summer he was half again as big and we took him back to the lake to let him go. We watched him swim away from us as if he hadn't missed a day. I was impressed that Oliver didn't show any trace of sentimental regret in letting his pet go free. He said it smiling, as if merely wishing him good luck: "Goodbye, Snappy!"*

I was fascinated by the depths of the lake but also afraid of them. In the dream image, it was the fear that stood out. Fear of what exactly? Of the snapping turtles? They were the real monsters of the lake. I was always afraid to let my bare feet touch the weedy, silted bottom for dread of being bitten.

Suddenly it all falls into place. I skated effortlessly over a dark, unknown depth. Don't I have to apply the analytic principle and suppose that the real terror, precisely the thing I most want to skate over, is something in myself? Isn't the real monster prowling in the depths my own hurt, and my own anger? Isn't that the lesson of shooting the turtle?

Barbara's silence seems like a confirmation. The black water is my own depth, its opacity is my own opacity. Beneath that inky surface is my own rage.

For a moment, I'm pulled up short by a wave of contempt for the whole apparatus of psychoanalysis. Haven't I fit myself all too neatly into the headshrinker's game? It seems like a caricature of analysis, a banality. Am I supposed to realize that shooting the turtle was a version of killing my father? My mind spins over a litany of Freud haters—Nabokov, for instance, or Gore Vidal—people who despised the pat formulas and crude themes in which Freud discerned the workings of the unconscious. Freud had his Ratman and his Wolfman. Are we to have a Turtleman as well? Isn't it all too formulaic, an overwrought exercise in navel-gazing?

Barbara still says nothing.

Then again, what is my own critical protest just now but an attempt to discount a painful discovery about myself, to blunt its impact, to stay blind to my own reality?

Elaine. She was a black lake. Much as I loved some things about her, I was forever supposing that there was a depth in her that I couldn't see into, some significant but unacknowledged interior that she withheld from me. I was always lured by the fantasy of unlocking some secret part of her that I'd never seen before. Access to it would flood her, and me, with some greater energy and vitality. It was—no question—the primary fantasy that shaped my relationship with her.

But now a doubt intrudes. Was that sense of something opaque and inaccessible in my ex-wife really a cover for my own need for opacity, the need to deny my own potential for anger and violence? Was my sense of something unknown in Elaine rooted in my own unknown depths? Did my own disavowed rage get tangled and obscured in my relationship with her? I had always thought that it was Elaine's inhibitions that were the biggest challenge to our marriage. But what if it was all along my own unresolved, unacknowledged personal fuck-ups that were the real problem? The question makes me dizzy.

And was it then my own confusion that so mystified Oliver? Did he sense that opacity in me? Was I a black lake for him?

*It's a Sunday morning and he's just come down from his bedroom, clad only in pajama bottoms. His nine-year-old torso is lithe and pale. I'm immersed in reading over my morning coffee but he seems determined to distract and annoy me. He capers back and forth, ignoring my several attempts at a scolding word. Then, the coffee spills. Without thinking, I slap him. He shrinks away, the tears coming fast. The blow leaves a red, guilty hand print on his belly. Elaine vainly tries to console me. You didn't mean to hit him.*

More than once Rebecca has remarked about my lack of anger at him in the aftermath of his death. A telling lack? There's certainly no shortage of things to be furious about. Traumatizing Jack with his rages, of course, but also the capital fact of shooting himself. The ultimate act of aggression, and not just against himself. What a terrible thing to do to Anna. In the middle of an argument in which she is laying down her minimal expectations for your behavior—pretty reasonable expectations, actually—you go in the next room and blow your brains out?

I fall silent. A long, tense quiet. I'm sure that Barbara will ask me about my dropping into the second person, as though I were talking directly to him.

Her voice comes even more quietly than usual. "That's all for today," she says.

# *15*

Yesterday's session was a big one. I still feel its impact physically, as if I've taken a blow. As I lie down again on the couch, I feel like a prizefighter flopping onto the corner stool and leaning back against the ropes.

Barbara seemed more assertive yesterday. Was it her revenge on me for having strayed into the psilocybin study? I know she didn't like it. And it's true that my impulse to join the study was in some part a mini-rebellion, a way of sidestepping the torture rack of her analyst's couch. It even occurred to me to wonder whether it was an echo of my old penchant for withdrawing to the treetop. Yet it seemed less aimed directly at her than at the frustrating slowness of the whole analytic process. Either way, her responses last time felt a bit more pointed, more forceful.

That sense seems confirmed when she immediately returns to the dream of the black lake, as if the break of the past twenty-four hours never occurred.

"Any thoughts about the second part of the dream, the part where you saw the cottage renovated by the new owners?"

I'm again gratified that she remembers the details of the dream, though again I feel ambushed and discomfited by her question.

It's an elemental contrast: dark to light. The black of the lake depths versus the light of the gigantic windows of the renovated cottage. But what really struck me was the ambitiousness, even aggressiveness, of the new owners in dismantling and reconstructing the place.

It was as if the new owners wielded a productive, no-holds-barred, creative energy, making dramatic changes that my family had been somehow too timid to attempt. Even the smallest details seem to confirm it. The trap-door in the back kitchen, for example. The new owners found a passageway to some depth of the house that was unknown to me. Or the low railings on the porch, as if to emphasize that the cottage was separated from the lake and its mysteries by the most minimal possible barrier.

The dream seems to cast my own family as overly cautious, unable to act on their ambitions. And then I remember. That's exactly what my grandfather confessed on his deathbed. His greatest regret, he told my father, was that he hadn't been more ambitious.

Was that the whole secret of Turner? To return to Maine, the rural, sparsely populated, northeastern corner of the country. What better place to take refuge? An idyllic cottage at the end of a long, dirt road in the Maine woods. Wasn't that the perfect escape from a larger, more challenging world? My head spins at the thought: was the camp at Turner my grandfather's version of my perch in the treetop?

It fits with other things I know. After the crash in 1929, stung by his sense of having lost a lot of other people's money, Gramp quit the bank in St. Louis and returned to Maine to take a less demanding job in the shoe industry. And then— yes, of course!—my father took exactly the same path. More than once I'd heard the story about the day my twenty-one-year-old father came home—it was just after the war—and announced that he'd been offered a job at the Casco Bank in Portland. My grandmother was over the moon. "Of course, Dickie, that's just the thing for you! You know your father was once in banking." But my grandfather immediately voiced doubts. Why not join him in the shoe company?

Dick and Dickie had always shared an extraordinarily close bond. But going into the shoe business was a choice my father always regretted. It was a job he always hated. I remember him during his years as the factory superintendent at Holmes & Stickney in Portland, lying prostrate on the couch in the evenings with terrible headaches and bouts of indigestion.

Maybe that explains my crying in the dream. Crying over feeling trapped in passive impotence. Crying because I found myself unable to wield any real force, unable to access the energy of an independent assertiveness. Crying to realize something deeply painful about my own place in the string of Richards.

"But you're leaving something out."

Her voice startles me. It again strikes me that she's intervening more forcefully than usual.

"It is you yourself who have renovated the cottage. It's your dream that has done that."

She's right of course. The dream presents the dramatic transformation of the cottage as accomplished by the new owners. But it was, after

all, *my* dream. The changes are mine. Why didn't
I think of that?

Then another childhood memory of Turner
lights up. Am I eight? Nine? We were once again
trying to put some order into the chaos of the
old garage. Among other things that needed
attending to was a squirrels' nest, a great tangle of
shredded newspaper, leaves, and wads of mattress
stuffing in one of the big wooden boxes under the
workbench. Beneath the fuzz ball of the nest, the
box contained a number of massive iron bolts,
remnants of the old windmill. My father assigned
me the job of cleaning it out.

Vaguely disgusted by the nest itself and anxious
to find a quick and easy way to get rid of it, I hit
upon the idea of setting it on fire. The tinder-
dry fluff of the nest would burn away leaving the
heavy iron bolts neatly behind. Simple enough.
Ingenious, actually! But my plan goes dangerously
awry, above all because I neglect to move the box
out of the garage before lighting it on fire. A few
moments later, my father, my grandfather, and
my brother turn with horror to see flames leaping
out of the wooden box, a five-gallon jerry can

of gasoline not more than six feet away, and me
paralyzed with terror.

At the time, the incident helped crystallize my
sense of myself as the Martian of the family. But
set beside the dream of the rebuilt cottage, it
also hints at a destructive impulse that I've never
before admitted to myself. In effect, didn't I set
fire to the place?

I'm more and more having to recognize that the
whole complex of Turner memories, my whole
experience of the place, was animated by tensions
that I've never acknowledged. I thought again of
the fires Oliver and I shared years later on the
Picnic Grounds.

"The turtles and the fires. That's where we began."

Yes, turtles and fires. Both now seem like stand-
ins for my complicated relationship to anger,
aggression, and ambition. The insight is deeply
gratifying, a breakthrough I've worked hard
for. But—I don't know why—it also makes me
deeply miserable. My whole body is tense. My
hands in fists.

Driving home, I think of Oliver.

*Unlike me, he was a born dancer. Dancing was in his bones, or maybe better, his capacity for fluid motion made it hard to believe he had any bones. As a toddler, he would twirl and swoop, eyes closed, drunk with sound to the point of crashing into walls and furniture, as if the pure pulse of rhythm swept him beyond concern for mere details like gravity. In his teens he smoothed a broad repertoire of moves, honing a lexicon with which at any moment he could write a marvelous body poetry in space.*

The most charming thing about Oliver as a child was his magical spark of enthusiasm for exploring. Deb Azrael, a student in my first discussion section as a teaching assistant in graduate school and who lived just down the street from us in Somerville, was instantly delighted by it when she met him. Oliver was the proverbial kid in a candy store, squealing wide-eyed at the world. Deb more than once protested against being paid for her hours of babysitting, as she took such pleasure in his company. During the last few years of my graduate work, they enjoyed regular adventures together—trooping around Harvard Square, circling Fresh Pond, even hopping on the subway for various sites in Boston.

*It's the first time he's ever been out in the snow, on the sidewalk in front of our place on Cleveland Street. He's dancing with the descending flakes, twirling with his two-year-old arms outstretched, his eyes closed, squinting in delight for the icy kisses of the crystals on his face. Then he's running in circles, his arms still out wide, as if to test the resistance of this magic shower-swirl of white, as if he might find it solid enough to push off from. As if he might take flight himself.*

In pursuit of his youthful interests, Oliver would throw himself into things with abandon, showing nothing of my native tentativeness. But in the last tough years of his addiction, he was increasingly, if sometimes disastrously, decisive. It was in that spirit that he attacked the project of launching his fledgling roofing business, buying tools and a truck, lining up jobs, advertising around town. It was the same resolute, risk-taking spirit that energized his decisiveness about Jack's birth.

Had the same poker player's "all-in" attitude that led him to extremes also taken him over the cliff in his relation to drugs in the first place? Oliver did nothing halfway. Lack of ownership of his own more violent energies was not his problem.

But does that mean—is it possible?—that he assumed a ferocity of decisiveness and a force of assertion that I refused?

Was that the meaning of my tears in the dream? Was Oliver caught in the grip of a disavowed rage I passed on to him? Was he the victim of a denial that I never worked out for myself?

The same crazy question keeps coming back. Was the bullet that I had fired into the head of that turtle, the act that I seem to have spent my life denying, the bullet that finally killed my son?

# *16*

I've always harbored a secret cynicism about
funerals. The proximity of death seems to
unhinge people's intelligence, forcing them
to take refuge in empty formalities and vapid
sentimentality. Who scripted this little list of
worn-out, even nonsensical comments? "He's
at peace now" is a favorite. Or, for the more
devout, "God has called him home." Then there
is the standard "I'm sorry," a remark I've always
regarded as particularly silly. In what sense or
for what reason do people offer an apology in the

face of death? Are they responsible? The best I can think of, giving it my most generous benefit of a doubt, is that they are apologizing for existence itself, making excuses for the cruel order of things that demands death and inflicts it upon us so capriciously. It is as if they are saying, "I'm sorry that the world is constructed in such a way that we all eventually have our guts ripped out; that if you live long enough, you live to see everything you love torn from you. I don't know why it must be so, but I'm deeply sorry that it is."

As Rebecca and I leave the house for the service, I'm bracing myself for a deluge of such paeans of sympathetic inanity. I'm all the more guarded for the depth of the wound I'm carrying. What can anyone say to me that could offer the slightest consolation? I am basically dreading the whole affair.

But when we enter the funeral home, a place whose name—Peaceful Alternatives—had already given me cause to expect the worst, I am immediately and completely upended. Even upon our arrival, almost an hour before the ceremony is to begin, a large crowd has gathered; close friends and family, but also dozens of my colleagues from the university, some of them people I know only in passing. Many of the people I don't know at all, mostly high school friends of Oliver's and their parents. I hadn't expected anything of the sort. The room in which we are to conduct the service can seat 180—plenty and then some, I had thought, to accommodate the mourners for Oliver's funeral. But the room is already almost full. I suddenly feel an absurd sense of panic, as if, in planning an event with insufficient space, I've made a promise that I can't deliver.

And they just keep coming. By the appointed hour, the place is crammed with people standing in the aisles and in the back, overflowing in large numbers into the hallway outside the room. The energizing effect amazes and astonishes me. Old friends and complete strangers come up and hug me. Their repetitions of "I'm sorry, I'm so, so sorry," feel like the sweetest imaginable balm, touching me at a depth that I had not thought possible. I am completely overwhelmed with gratitude. The crowd must be three hundred or more.

The deep fatigue and despair of the week melts away and in its place I feel renewed by a surge of strength. My prior misgivings about the funeral shame me, though even that shame is washed away in the face of the outpouring of support and sympathy. To my surprise and immense relief, I manage to get through the eulogy I had written for him without hopelessly breaking down.

Looking back on it, I'm happy that I spoke directly about his suicide. To not mention it seemed out of the question. In fact, I was inclined to ask whether his pulling the trigger wasn't a thoughtless, selfish act after all. What if, feeling himself trapped in an addiction that he could not overcome, he finally did the only thing that he knew how to do? Maybe, in that final, bitter moment, he chose to spare those he loved the agony of his own losing battle. Maybe he chose to free his family from the violence and ugliness of his own struggle, even at the price of his own life.

Is that right? Of course, I will never know for sure. But I was happy to give him the benefit of the doubt. It was a conclusion that tallied with what I knew of his heart.

The end of the ceremony was sublimely moving, as we asked the gathering of people to come forward to light tea candles on the long, cloth-draped table on which we'd placed the container of Oliver's ashes, cradled by a simple bier of evergreen sprigs and flowers. As the last of the crowd slowly filed out, the table was aglow with hundreds of little flames, washing the front of the room with a gentle brilliance that was as haunting as it was beautiful.

The service concluded with a Native American prayer, one that I found scrawled on a piece of paper lying on the table beside Oliver's bed.

*Grandfather, Great Spirit, Master of all things,*
*You who are called by so many names,*
*And worshipped in so many ways;*
*Allow me to become the Earth,*
*Teach me to surrender to the tracks,*
*So that I may become that which I follow,*
*And if I am worthy, allow these tracks*
*to lead me closer to You.*

*Stalking Wolf, Apache Elder*

# 17

I'm pretty sure that my second experience with psilocybin was a lower dose. Still thrilling and fascinating, though without the full-throttle psychosis of the first go-around. Yet both of the first two sessions were somewhat predictable. Not to diminish the impact of the dizzying hallucinations, the superintense emotion of the music, the bizarre melting of reality. The drug unquestionably delivered some of the most powerful and meaningful experiences of my life. I emerged feeling altered and enriched in ways that beggar description. It now makes perfect sense to me that various peoples have relied on psychedelic substances to enable radical experiences of spiritual growth and change. But, all that said, the first two sessions still more or less fit my rough, admittedly somewhat Hollywood image of dropping acid.

The third dose was something else. The drug seemed to hijack a different part of my brain. Where the first two trips seemed comparable to hypervivid dreams, the third was more purely cerebral. It was once again an immense soul explosion, but it was triggered less by sensations or emotions than by pure ideas. The result completely exceeded my wildest expectations.

Once again, I have shortened and sharpened my original report, but what follows is the core account I wrote during the week following the session.

### Notes on the Third Psilocybin Session, February 9, 2007

I have tried to resist the temptation to edit or interpret my memory of the experience, recording my impressions exactly as they occurred to me. As I've worked on writing them up during the past week, I have at times been almost embarrassed by them, as if they indulge a cosmic vision of the triumph of love that one associates with the saccharine platitudes of Hallmark cards. All the same, the basic insights opened up during the session still seem very compelling to me.

Despite my suspicion that for the third session I received a lesser dose than the first, its effect was much greater. I felt at the time and continue to feel that it produced the most deeply significant and beautiful experience of my life. The reason didn't have to do with the play of visual hallucinations, though the light show, especially early on, was even more breathtaking than in either of the previous doses. The distinctive and compelling experience of this session was a series of overwhelming intuitions, what I can only describe, despite my lack of any coherent religious belief, as revelations. It felt like I was glimpsing some ultimate vision of reality.

Each of those visions was accompanied by a sense of great mystery, the humbling feeling of a great deal more to be known, as if I were barely glimpsing some infinite dimension. Yet each revelation also flooded me with a sense of deep conviction. For some extended period, I felt paralyzed, not by any physical inability to move but rather by the ecstasy of the revelations themselves. Each new vision came with a double rush of stunned wonder and intense pleasure. I couldn't bear to disturb their flow.

Once again, I was acutely aware of the dramatic effects when I relaxed while experiencing the drug. When I would tighten and anxiously resist, the visual field would flatten, darken, and contract. Dense geometric patterns buzzed with filigrees of colored light in a way that was interesting but also unpleasant. Yet as soon as I allowed myself to relax, letting my shoulders sink back into the couch with an exhalation of breath, consciously letting my abdomen soften and relax, the space before my eyes would yawn open and ever more enormous shapes and surfaces would unfurl, illuminated by thrilling sweeps of light. The onset of revelatory experiences, too, seemed to correspond to whatever success I had in staying relaxed.

That art of relaxation itself triggered the first great wave of revelation, as it suddenly seemed obvious to me that maintaining precisely such an attitude, a trusting and loving openness of spirit, is the very essence and purpose of life. Our task in life consists in letting go of fear in order to purely give ourselves to the impact of the present. We are called to make ourselves open to experience without prejudice or judgment. We are therefore essentially explorers, whose task is to venture out into new experiences. I thought again of Mary's metaphor of the astronaut, the sole witness shot out into space in the service of seeing what no one has ever seen before.

Then I find myself mindful of the enormous community of people required to launch just one person into space. The hundreds of engineers and ground crew, of course, but also the other nameless crowds who smelt the metals, assemble the myriad component parts, and forge the gantries and scaffolds that will steady the rocket; as well as the ones who produce and load the fuels, who grow and pack the foods, who sew the space suit and shape the helmet, etc. Then, too, there are the untold thousands of researchers and theorists—centuries of astronomers, mathematicians, and physicists—without whom no one of us could ever escape the hold of gravity. It is a vision of a great interconnected web of humanity engaged in an unfolding cosmic adventure.

It then strikes with enormous force: *all of us are such astronauts.* We are all such privileged explorers, each on our own, unique journey, launched by an immense network of other people. That network most obviously includes one's family, but also the larger community that helps sustain families, the nation and larger culture that supports and nourishes communities, and finally the past generations without whose contributions the present could not exist. Every moment of our life experience is made possible by a great skein of others, most of whom we've never met.

While still aswim in this vision, an even larger realization rushes over me about the nature of God. The usual understanding poses the divine as the endpoint, the destination of all cosmic journeying, the grand goal toward which we are struggling. We are pilgrims on our way toward God, helped along at points by gifts of grace. Following a trail of crumbs strewn by God's hand, we will eventually arrive at His side.

The correction hits like a violent gust of wind. God is not the destination, but the animating spirit of the journey itself. God exists only in and through the passage. The truth, at once confounding and exhilarating, is that God is not a completed, self-enclosed being, waiting eternally at the far side of some immense void. On the contrary, God Himself is a work in progress, Himself energized by the force of love and longing. Even God doesn't know in advance what we will find on our voyage. And it is a matter of *we*. God isn't waiting for us at a distance. He is right beside us. Or better, *inside* us. God sees with our eyes, hears with our ears, feels through our hearts. God *comes to be* through our seeing, hearing, and feeling—if only we really do see, and hear, and feel. The ultimate astronaut, the ultimate explorer, the ultimate pilgrim embarked on a strange journey of revelation, is God Himself.

Even as this thought train is coursing through my mind I am weirdly aware—as if able to maintain some shred of a critical, academic distance from my own unfolding psychosis—that this latest "revelation" isn't just a minor departure from orthodox dogma but an insight into the most radical possible theology. Contrary to the received view of God as the eternal, unchanging Substance, it is a vision of an incomplete God, the spirit of perfect openness to existence, the heartbeat of love in an unfolding drama of pure and infinite possibility. Simultaneous with this dizzying awareness, an epiphany of really remarkable beauty and wonder, some part of me is also able to stand at a bemused distance. This, I think, chuckling to myself, is what decades of reading philosophy looks like on acid!

But then the whole torrent of realizations again suddenly shifts. Did my chuckling disturb it? The whole God theme somehow intersects with another series of thoughts about Oliver that had been unfolding all the while along some parallel track.

Early in the session, he returned to me with extraordinary clarity and impact, and I had the thought—totally strange, but completely convincing—that Oliver is the only absolutely pure thing I know. I felt swept up into a perfect intuition of his heart and essence. I had experienced a hint of this miraculous recovery in the immediate aftermath of his death. The real core of his person seemed to float free from its entanglement with all of the ugliness, pain, and cruelty of his struggle with addiction. I tried to describe it in my eulogy at the funeral. Now, under the influence of the drug, I feel completely swept up into an intimate connection with Oliver's essential personality. At the same time, I am overcome with the paradox that it is only in the event of his death that I am able to recontact him. How astonishing and terrifying, how deeply wounding, that he should return to me only when he is irretrievably lost.

Feeling poised on the edge of an abyss, an unthinkable mix of joy and pain, a string of further revelations flow into each other, building toward some kind of crescendo. The first wave is realizing that in some bizarre way Oliver seems more present to me in his absence, that he has come alive in his death, that I have been returned to him and him to me only in the moment of losing him.

Then the whole series of reflections from the theological and philosophical tradition seems to converge in a great unity, the main point of which is how the ultimate mystery resides in the heart of death and loss. Death, loss, failure—all of the faces of negation—are not at all what they first appear to be. Far from being moments of closure and finality, the moment of death is the moment of opening. It is only when the door is finally and

irrevocably shut that it opens. If we are receptive
to it in the right way, there truly is no death,
for the loved one who has died reappears to us,
strangely, as if in a kind of peripheral vision, yet
even more powerfully and more purely than when
they appeared in life. What comes to us from the
hinterland of death is the spiritual core of the
departed person, distilled and purified by the
passage into death.

In the midst of this unfolding rush, I begin
to feel overloaded with the sheer number and
enormity of visions, as if I won't be able to tolerate
any more. But I can't turn away from them either.
On the contrary, the whole movement seems
only to accelerate. I even have the sense of being
able to pose questions, merely mouthing them to
the void, to which answers almost immediately
present themselves. In a climactic epiphany, love
appears as the inner essence of everything. The
journey of spirit coming to itself, revealing its own
inner mystery, is nothing but the self-realization
of love.

Like a plant that must be severely pruned in
order to stimulate its most luxuriant blossoming,
love requires its own ongoing tragedy to unfold
the fullness of its beauty. This realization of love

takes place in the interior of our own souls, where nothing is completely lost.

It was, among other things, a vision into the true nature of forgiveness, both of others and of oneself. All of love's wounds and disappointments, in others and ourselves, are finally taken up and redeemed in a greater whole. And this, precisely because love needs its failures, love needs death. It is only in death that love comes into the openness of its absolute purity. It feels like a completely new insight into the old adage that "love conquers all."

I have no idea how long this hurricane of revelations lasted. It might have been an extra-intense fifteen minutes. It might have taken three hours. But once returned to the "real world," I felt limp from the passing storm. Hurricane is a good metaphor. For several days afterward, I felt like the bent and shredded palm trees on a storm-wracked beach. Yet true to the psychedelic paradox, I also felt strangely focused and relaxed.

What, then, to make of it all? It was not without its comic side, one that I remember enjoying even in the midst of it. At one point, like a kind of involuntary joke at my own expense, the image passed through my mind of the old antidrug TV spot from the 1980s in which a hen's egg—"This is your brain"—is cracked and dropped into a sizzling frying pan—"This is your brain on drugs!"

Mildly comic, while also being true to type. After my own experience, doing the sort of background reading that academics find irresistible, I learned that mystical visions like the ones I had are quite typical of the psilocybin experience. It is not for nothing that psilocybin and its family of psychotropic substances are sometimes called Entheogens—"See God" drugs.

That mystical, mind-exploding power of psychedelics was the prime source of their appeal to the Woodstock generation, but it also fired interest among serious researchers in the 1960s whose work produced remarkably promising results. Sadly, virtually all of that research was buried and forgotten after Richard Nixon's 1971 declaration of the "war on drugs." Only recently and in a few quiet corners has that kind of scientific study been taken up again, including in the work of Roland Griffiths at Hopkins. Aside from the focus on spirituality in the protocol that I participated in, Griffiths and his team have produced striking outcomes using psilocybin with people struggling to quit smoking, coping with depression or obsession, as well as dealing with the fear and anguish of terminal cancer diagnoses. My own experience makes me wonder if severe grief might not usefully be added to that list.

Among neuroscientists, the extraordinary effects of drugs like psilocybin are attributed to the way they affect the inhibitory system of the brain, the so-called default mode network. The network's function is to establish a stable sense of self, clearly separating ego from non-ego, subject from object. Under the influence of the drug, things that would otherwise be securely held apart, enabling the sense of an ordered and coherent world, melt into one another as the drug short-circuits disparate swaths of the brain's synaptic web. The resulting experience, felt to be vividly, even unquestionably real, is quite typically one of the ultimate unity, beauty, and perfection of all things.

The problem, of course, is whether the familiar, everyday world without drugs, the world in which a practical-minded, stabilizing ego identity keeps the keel under the boat, can claim to be the "true" reality. On the contrary, isn't it rather a dimmed-down and flattened version of life that just makes it all easier to cope with? A good question for a philosopher if ever there was one.

To make the same point from another angle, the challenging fact is that the fantastic vision triggered by psilocybin corresponded with uncanny accuracy and gut-level certainty to some core reality of my own life experience. It was impossible not to feel that the psychedelic whirlwind made far better sense of my world than I had ever managed to do without it.

Or was it a matter of merely wishing it were so?

# 18

Toward the end of today's session with Barbara, an odd memory pops into mind. Oliver had just turned nineteen. It was a year and a half before he moved in with Becky and me, almost four years before his suicide. He was living with me for a while in my little apartment on Maryland Avenue. He was thumbing through the pages of a book of mine in which I wrote about the religious and psychological dimensions of sacrifice.

"Dad," he asked, "what's this sacrifice thing?"

I spoke briefly about the way that sacrifice enacts a deliberate wasting of something, attempting to engage divine powers by intentionally destroying something of value. For many cultures, I said, the sacred enters the world in the place vacated by death.

Oliver's reaction was immediate. "That's what I am," he said. "I'm the wasted thing. I'm a sacrifice. I've wasted my life in drugs."

My shock at this pronouncement only deepened as he elaborated on it.

"I've wasted my talents," he said. "I've wasted my time. I've wasted my mind. I've thrown away my hopes and my future. And I've done it deliberately. That's why I had to go to heroin. That was the most extreme thing, the most totally wasting thing."

"But why, Oliver? Why did you have to do that?"

"I don't know," he said. He paused for a moment, then said something that stunned me.

"I think I had to become a heroin addict because it was Mom's worst fear," he said. "I think I had to do the thing that she was most afraid of."

My reaction bordered on complete disbelief. How and why did he so immediately recognize himself as a sacrifice? And what could it possibly mean that he needed to realize his mother's worst fear? I tried to pursue it with him for the next few minutes, but we didn't make much headway. I lamely attempted to put a positive spin on it, suggesting that maybe he needed to sink to some depth, to waste or purge something in himself, before getting a new start. Maybe he would eventually move on and regrasp his life. But he didn't offer much of a response and we wandered off the topic.

That conversation haunted me in the wake of his death. Was his suicide the culmination of some self-sacrificial impulse? I thought of Iphigenia, the daughter of Agamemnon, whose sacrifice was required to release the winds that drove the

Achaean ships to Troy. Was Oliver's life and death, in its own way, a tragic transmission of crime and guilt?

The whole catastrophe seems momentarily to rise up in a new and unexpected way. The fall of the house of Atreus began with the adultery of Thyestes. Was Oliver caught up in the unfolding of some parallel drama? Was my own adultery, the crime that he himself discovered, the fatal trigger of his destruction?

It's a strange and excruciating moment. I'm embarrassed by the grandiose framing that I'm giving the whole story—my life as Homeric epic—but I can't help feeling that I've finally disentangled the threads of my own part in Oliver's death, a part that I suspected and feared, yet that I've been neither fully able to articulate nor fully willing to admit. It feels like I've finally sunk to the bottom of my own lake of tears.

I had earlier come to the idea of Oliver enacting a force of rage that belonged originally to me, as if he circuited an energy against which I put up a strenuous internal resistance. What if the precise point at which that rage was triggered in him was the discovery of my infidelity?

Barbara listens to all this without comment and I'm increasingly pained by her silence. Meanwhile, my own thoughts keep moving.

If this view is right, wouldn't it account for his stubborn resistance to therapy? Oliver was caught up in a story not entirely his own, a story he couldn't tell even if he wanted to. Is it even possible that his resistance to therapy was rooted in an obscure impulse to protect me, to spare me having to face the ways that I had disappointed him? The thought makes me feel sick. Is it possible that the love between us became so exquisitely and terribly knotted? Is that possible?

Barbara says nothing for a moment, as if pausing to make sure that I'm really expecting an answer to my question.

"Having never met or spoken with Oliver, there's not much I can say about that."

Yes, but you're a therapist, I'm just asking whether you think it's a likely scenario.

"You want me to speculate."

I'm impatient with her refusal to answer what seems to me a simple question.

Barbara says nothing.

I can't help feeling—I have a hard time getting my breath—I can't help feeling that I've reached a sort of bedrock of the whole terrible history.

"You are again wondering about your own guilt."

Yes, I'm asking about my guilt. And why not? I know the whole psychoanalytic shtick about guilt, about how the progress of analysis is supposed to lighten the patient's self-punishment. But this doesn't feel like neurotic guilt. In fact, this whole labor of analysis seems, if anything, to have increased my sense of guilt. It has revealed my dodges and self-deceits. It's stripped me of a whole battery of comforting illusions. It's denied me my usual aesthetic and intellectual distractions. I feel like Oedipus. He sets out to find his father's murderer and finds himself. Hasn't my own effort to find the truth of Oliver's death led to my own part in it?

I hear Barbara take a half breath and I find myself waiting eagerly to hear what she's about to say, hoping for some resolution, some enlightening remark that releases the tension. Some verdict or some benediction.

"That's all the time we have for today," she says.

Driving home from my session, mulling over the results, I find myself rethinking the whole course of my analysis. When I first started with Barbara, quite apart from the desire to learn what I could about myself and my own possible role in my son's death, I also simply needed someone to talk to. One of the stranger things about intense grief is its loneliness, its terrible feeling of isolation. It is as if mourning saddles us with a deep conviction of our own unworthiness, our own unfitness for human contact. The result is that, just when we most desperately need companionship, we cannot tolerate it. In the depths of grief, we become untouchables, somehow wounded not just by the loss of the one we loved, but by an inexplicable feeling of shame. The gauntlet of mourning makes lepers of us all.

It's the reason why attending group meetings with other grief-stricken people can be so deeply consoling. Who but they can understand our depth of agony? Yet even in such groups, speaking can be searingly difficult, as if sharing our pain, even with others who are equally lacerated by it, only deepens our feeling of unworthiness. My own solution was to pay someone to listen to me, to bear the burden of my sobbing.

And yet, despite my own doubts, the work of the analysis has clearly succeeded in breaking into the basement of my soul and turning over the furniture. The dream of the black lake still makes me shiver. It now seems deeply appropriate that the blackness of the depths in the dream brought together the darkness of my grief with a darkness of rage I had always hidden from myself. I knew that recovering the memory of killing the turtle was a deeply pivotal moment.

Yet it now seems clear that its power lay less in releasing the emotional impact of the memory itself than in opening the interpretation of the black lake.

I owe that breakthrough to Barbara's intervention. At the time, I felt something new from her, an unexpected pointedness in her comment, as if she had finally seen her moment to strike and took it. Her brief, well-aimed questions had stunning impact. The miraculous effect was as immediate as it was game-changing. All she needed to do was to repeat what I had already spoken but had myself been unwilling to hear. The black lake was a part of me. I was skating over something in myself. And the violent renovation of the cottage, too, was my doing. I was refusing to admit my own act, failing to own a transformative violence that belonged to me. The flood of consequences then came on by itself, with an energy of its own.

A further realization then hits me. Stubbornly insisting on my own guilt in the session today was a way of pushing back against those consequences. Even in the midst of it, I vaguely felt like I was overdoing my own guilt trip. I was all too ready to be annoyed at Barbara's unwillingness to give me a simple answer to what seemed like a simple question. I had set her up for it. It's hard not to think that I was taking some measure of revenge on her for cornering me in the cramped space of my own neurotic alibi.

Wrapping myself in a guilty self-accusation was a way of regaining some measure of control, of reasserting that I could be my own master, making myself responsible for everything. Whatever the pain of feeling guilty, it was preferable to the deeply destabilizing realizations of the past few sessions on Barbara's couch. Better to whip myself with guilt than to own up to the fact that my own sense of myself has always conspired with a deep self-deception. I've denied my own capacity for violence. No wonder I want to accuse myself. In an important sense, I've deceived myself all my life. I've been living a kind of fiction that I invented.

As I collapse into the reading chair in my study, still mulling over the results of the session, the fog of doubt around my self-accusation only thickens. So far, the analysis has taught me a series of profound lessons about myself, lessons that feel as deeply correct as they are deeply wrenching—that feel correct precisely because they're so wrenching. But am I right to use those insights as keys to my son's life and death? What real evidence is there to decide one way or the other?

Then again, even if big parts of the story I've come to are right, is it the whole story? If Oliver got entangled in tensions internal to his relation with me—and surely some of that is true—it's equally true that there was a whole series of other contingencies that figured in the final outcome of things.

I still don't know, and cannot know, what innate factors may have played a hand in the unfolding of Oliver's drug abuse. Drug counselors and medical professionals point to the organic bases of addiction. Some argue that roughly ten percent of the population is genetically predisposed. Was his early experimenting with drugs like lighting the fuse on a genetic bomb?

Or was he all the while self-medicating an underlying psychological disorder? More than once we were told that his psychological state suggested bipolar disorder, but that a reliable diagnosis couldn't be made in the midst of his active substance abuse. Was his suicide a consequence of untreated manic depression?

There is also his own part in it all. Doesn't he have to bear some responsibility for his flawed choices? Rebecca has more than once wondered whether Oliver used his anger at me over the breakup with his mother as a blind behind which he hid his own failures, especially his dependence on drugs.

Then there is the circle of kids he fell in with during his middle and high school years and their problematic base of operations. Unbeknownst to the other parents of that group, including Elaine and me, the mother of one of Oliver's best friends had settled on the devil's bargain of allowing the gang to drink and smoke weed at her home, as long as they did it outside the house somewhere. She consoled herself with the thought that at least they'd be doing it in a relatively safe place, free from the risks of car accidents or getting arrested. Of course, that house became their constant hangout. Of that group of fifteen or twenty kids, an alarming number developed serious drug problems. Fully six of them ended up using heroin. One died of an overdose and two, Oliver and another boy, ended up killing themselves. That other boy hanged himself in the family garage.

It's only recently that I've connected the dots around a bigger, darker consideration. Like so many thousands of Americans in the recent explosion of opioid addiction, Oliver trod a path to becoming a heroin junkie that passed through Oxycontin. When we returned from his promising but ultimately botched time at Teen Care Camp, he almost immediately fell into a dependency on Oxycontin, the powerfully addictive drug aggressively advertised by Purdue Pharma as non-habit-forming. After his very first pill, he later told Elaine, a dose stolen for him by a friend whose grandmother was taking it to kill the pain of a terminal cancer, he knew he would never want any other drug. The streets were flooded with Oxy in the early 2000s, but it was expensive. Once he was hooked, which didn't take long, Oliver did what thousands of other Oxy addicts did. He transferred to the far cheaper, more readily available equivalent: heroin. One could easily argue that what ultimately drove my son over the edge was the greed and deceit of the Sackler family. Even now, after the bankruptcy of their drug company, they retain most of their billions in profits from peddling their deadly pills.

How am I to put my own contribution to Oliver's difficulties into proper relation with those other factors? I don't know. I can't know.

The deep lake of unknowing came back when I finally held the gun with which he'd killed himself. After more than a year of being held in evidence by the police, I finally arranged for its return. I had been unable to tolerate the idea of it becoming the property of some anonymous person, oblivious to its history as the instrument of my son's death. For that and other reasons that remained obscure to me, it seemed an absolute necessity to get it back. Yet I was apprehensive about the moment that I would actually see the thing, and my response to it when the time came took me completely by surprise.

As I took the pistol out of its case and held it in my hands, I was washed over by an enormous wave of feeling that I can only describe as love. Though one might easily imagine that I would regard the hateful thing with rage and disgust, perhaps even be moved to take my revenge on it by hammering it to pieces, I held the gun with the exaggerated tenderness of a mother cradling a newborn baby. Was it merely because it was the last thing that Oliver touched? Was it a rush of sympathy having nothing to do with the pistol itself, whose last firing had taken my son's life, but rather for the way that it recalled the final, dreadful moment of his life in which, alone and despairing, he pulled the trigger? Or was it that holding the gun with which he had shot himself to death aroused in me a moment of heartrending forgiveness? I don't know.

One might well think that these uncertainties would ease my mind, as if I might take some refuge in the thicket of such unknowns. But the truth is more nearly the opposite. The impossibility of knowing for sure how to parse the reality of what happened makes it all the more tormenting. Aside from the brutal fact of his death, that wall of the unknowable is the most awful thing about the whole terrible sequence of events.

It's a painful irony. The drive to understand that led me decades ago into a career teaching philosophy is being bent back upon itself in an anguished admission of ignorance. After Oliver's death, the demand to know pressed on me like a vise. If I had lost my son, if I was condemned to suffer that terrible wound, all the more I needed to understand how and why it happened. I was possessed by the necessity to figure it out. But that demand to know now seems up against an implacable limit. Nor is my unknowing related only to things outside myself. It also concerns the core realities of my own life.

The unfolding of the analysis has brought me to a much deeper knowledge of myself and of my relation to my son. And I don't doubt the correctness of much of that new insight. But all of it now also seems suspended amid agonizing uncertainties. Is this mix of knowing and unknowing an inevitable part of the outcome of psychoanalysis, or, for that matter, of any serious attempt at self-understanding? Is psychoanalysis finally a tragic art, a process of bringing us up against the foundations of our lives, the soul-shaping circumstances and relationships that have always been flawed or broken, but that are finally rooted in things that remain mostly unfathomable?

# *19*

Over the past months, to my surprise, I feel somewhat better. The long labor with Barbara seems to have helped me. How strange that some release from pain can come from such a painful process.

Which only points to a paradox. Having found a limited relief from pain, at certain moments I'm even more susceptible to it. The session this morning is among the most deeply wrenching I've had.

It begins with a vague sense of malaise and annoyance. Going on about a petty argument with Rebecca, I flounder most of the session, feeling trapped and frustrated. Then, as if out of nowhere, I'm pitched into a black agony over Oliver's suicide. Only toward the very end of the hour does it dawn on me—I had known it was approaching but had somehow let it slip out of my mind. It's the second anniversary of his death.

I leave Barbara's office weak-kneed. On the drive home I buy a pack of cigarettes. I haven't smoked for over a year. In the immediate aftermath, it was a welcome act of solidarity with him, as well as a senseless gesture of self-destructiveness. Apparently, there's still some part of me that's indifferent about living or dying.

Arriving back at the empty house, I spend more than an hour poring over old photographs of him, smoking the same chain of cigarettes that Elaine and I shared the night he died. Many of the pictures were taken at the lake in Turner. One shows him holding a painted turtle, the brim of his baseball cap jutting out over his ten-year-old face, his eyes fixed on the turtle as if waiting for it to impart some secret to him. In another, taken when he was perhaps fourteen, he looks back at me with a glance cast over his shoulder, his eyes alight with an unknown emotion. There is also a series of pictures from his trip to Nepal and Tibet, every one of them a glowing testimony to the wonderful time he spent there.

Then there are pictures of him holding Jack, the boy he loved so much in the last three years of his life. I see myself in those images, holding him as a toddler, and I think again of the mystery of the turning generations, how we take our place in a silent inheritance of love and hope for the future.

Seeing the photographs triggers new seizures of grief. Blinded by tears, I am momentarily excused from looking at them. But at length, half from exhaustion, half from the liberal dosing of nicotine, I fall into a series of quiet reflections.

My first and second years of mourning have been strange inversions of one another. During the first year, I was protected from the worst pain, as if by the numbness of shock, but tears flowed easily. Countless times I retreated to the solitude of my study and listened again to Elgar's "Nimrod," which I had chosen for the funeral. The result was always an agonizing but cathartic fit of sobbing. Those convulsions of tears always left in their wake a blessed moment of calm and repose.

During the second year the pain intensified, as if penetrating deeper into me, and yet I found it increasingly hard to cry. It made the second year twice as difficult. I was like a man wracked with nausea, exhausted by repeated bouts of vomiting, who suffers even more frightfully from dry heaves, his body still bent over with convulsive waves, yet unable to expel anything more. In that respect, this morning's outburst was an exception.

I think, too, of the analysis. I hesitated at the idea of undertaking a psychoanalysis in the midst of such grief. Would I be too crippled to really give myself to the unfolding of the process? Might I have been better off to see a grief counselor or join a bereavement group, something to help stanch the most immediate hemorrhage, leaving the heavy soul-searching for some other time?

It now seems like my mourning somehow fed the analysis. Grief continually disrupted my everyday life, constantly making ordinary involvements and tasks seem indifferent or even absurd. But if Oliver's death blasted away the present it also tore up the past, turning even the most pleasant memories upside down and inside out. Grief became the emotional engine of my meetings with Barbara, releasing a seemingly inexhaustible flow of memories and feelings from my earliest childhood.

It is no accident that this morning's eruption occurred on Barbara's couch. My two years with her have progressively undone my defenses, opening me up to the violence of my own feelings. Still, I am struck by the sheer magnitude of pain. For some time now, I've been coming closer to confronting the brute fact of his loss, the terrible permanence of his absence.

It took a long time to hit bottom. Strange as it may sound, the cold reality of his death now dwarfs the burden of guilt that I've been carrying. However much I've anguished over my sense of failure as a father, however much I feared that I might have been to blame for his death, the simple fact of losing him has been much more deeply excruciating. In fact, the discrepancy between the two confirms something that I'd glimpsed but never really accepted. It's not only that they are two different sources and kinds of pain. My torments over feeling responsible have actually protected me from an even more elemental wound of pure and simple loss.

The sense of guilt I've nursed and even clung to over the past two years has been a defense against a far deeper sadness. I've been sidestepping the most unmanageable pain by continually scribbling in a ledger of self-accusations. In blaming myself, at least I was able to do something. I was able to keep giving something to him, to keep loving him. Above all, I was able to keep myself at the center of things, to keep his relation to me uppermost.

Am I then innocent of his death? Of course not. I made terrible mistakes, no doubt more than I know. I will forever carry some burden of guilt, the warrant of which I don't know how to measure, but the reality of which I cannot deny. It is a burden that I alone will bear in the silence of my own soul. Yet it now seems clear to me that I've overinflated that guilt, holding on to it the way that a drowning man clings to a life ring in a stormy sea.

Am I deceiving myself in reassessing things this way? Am I letting myself off easy? I don't think so. In fact, far from welcoming a release from guilt, I'm strangely reluctant to let it go.

My guilt has been a sort of gift to him, a last
act of willing sacrifice, a means of holding
on. Now, strangely enough, losing my sense of
responsibility is itself something to be mourned.
The most truly agonizing thing now seems the
very opposite of self-blame. The most painful
thing is the knowledge that, at each turn of that
long and difficult road, I did the best I could for
him. But it wasn't enough.

It is both deeply gratifying and deeply
wounding to realize that through it all it was my
love for him that motivated me. It was in no small
part my love for him that tied me to my marriage
with Elaine. It was love that drove me to stick
with him over the long years of his addiction.
And it was love that fueled my sense of guilt over
his death. But death is the ultimate catastrophe
of love. Death is the most implacable of love's
wounds. The deepest agony of death is love's
inability to touch and be touched by what it loves.


The second anniversary has caught me off guard.
It's a Wednesday, a day free from my teaching
duties, and now, taking a deep breath, I wonder
how best to spend it. And suddenly it seems

obvious. I have to return to the banks of Loch Raven Reservoir, where we scattered a portion of his ashes on the day of the funeral. It is a place that he dearly loved, a place we'd been together many times. I rummage around to find again the little turtle box I had given to him so long ago, the one in which I carried a portion of his ashes for scattering after the funeral. I fill it a second time, drawn from the urn that I have not yet been able to part with.

It's a glorious day, a high, pure-blue sky overhead. I park my car in the lot of Peerce's Plantation, the restaurant where we gathered for the evening meal after his funeral. I then start down the long grassy slope to the water's edge. The strangeness of repetition envelops me, having trod the same ground two years earlier with the crowd of family and friends. But this time I'm alone. Caught up in the labor of preparing the ceremony and delivering the eulogy on the day of the funeral, worried about the particulars of the arrangements and about the others in attendance, I was in a curious way deprived of the experience. It now feels like I walk the ground for the first time. To bury him with my own hands.

Reaching the water's edge, I sit down and drink in the silence and beauty of the place. No wonder Oliver so loved this spot. The long tongue of grass that extends from the road to the water is walled on either side by great pines whose branches faintly tremble in the breath of air. The water's surface, barely ruffled, spreads before me like a great, shining mirror. The densely forested far shores are unbroken by human habitation. Time is suspended.

My mind slides over a long series of memories, the virtual photographs stored in the album of my heart. As they have been so often since his death, the images seem impossibly vivid, impossibly close to me. Many times over the past two years I have suffered that strange and contradictory coincidence of uncanny presence and tormenting absence, feeling him to be closer to me than my immediate physical surroundings, as if I were able to hear his breath in my ear, as if I could feel his hand on the back of my neck, and yet at the same time feeling him agonizingly separated from me behind the locked door of death.

The mystery of the thing is terrifying. Are we all, each in our own way, each by our own path, destined to arrive at this wrenching wish to retrieve what has been taken from us? If we live long enough, are we not all delivered into this agony of purified longing, all that is left to us by the ravages of loss?

I'm held in the whirl of these reflections for a time, but before long they begin to fade. And then, without thinking, without any specific intention, I find myself talking to him. I speak especially of our good times together and chuckle more than once in the midst of the little parade of memories. I feel momentarily buoyed up by an unexpected lightheartedness and a delicious sense of communion with him. I sit for a long time, floating, suspended in air, savoring that feeling of connection. The words flow easily. In some impossible way, they feel received.

The silence again enfolds me. To speak at all seems a violation of the stillness. The time has come to give his ashes over to the waters that he loved so much. Crushed in my fist, the chalky dust seems magically to reassume a physical solidity that feels deeply welcome, as if I can once again lay hold of him, feel his bodily weight and living mass. I can almost feel his heat. The harder

I squeeze, the more intimately I feel reconnected with him, and the more readily the tears flow, as if I, too, am being bodily squeezed by some enormous, invisible hand.

As I release my grip, what had only moments before felt firm and almost heavy seems to vanish. The ash sifts through my fingers and drops into the water below, streaking the gently lapping waves like feathers and settling on the bottom in delicate, white tendrils. As I remount the bank, turn, and look back at the water's edge, I'm gratified that the white halo of ashes is still visible beneath the surface.

The sigh of the wind in the pines behind me momentarily turns my head and I gaze up into the treetops, now golden with the slanting sun. The characteristic sweep of the white pine branches reminds me of our times at the lake in Maine.

Turning back to look a final time at the water, I am immediately dismayed that the ashes are gone. A stab of panic is a cold jolt. Am I so soon to lose that last bare trace of him? But no, I see that the ashes are still there, just obscured by the reflection on the water's surface cast by a solitary cloud that has drifted across the otherwise uninterrupted blue vault to the south during the time that I was distracted by the trees. My heart warms at this little transubstantiation, the white of the ashes fused with the whiteness of the cloud, tracing the cycle of all water on our lovely planet, completing the mysterious circuit of life and death, death and new life.

Walking back over the grass to the road, overcome with a sense of intense intimacy with him, and of gratitude for its having been given to me, I feel poised at the perfect juncture of life and death. In the two years since his suicide I've been dominated by the sense of my own inner devastation, the field of wreckage inside myself. I've been acutely aware of not wanting to repair it, not wanting it to heal. Continuing to dwell amidst that inner wasting has been my last way of holding on to the boy I loved so much. I now inhabit that place of darkness and quiet, the place of death, a void of silence. I can now only think in that space, can only breathe in that space. And strangely, impossibly, that very darkness now seems like a source of strength and renewal.

Somewhere in the brokenness of my soul a new life is slowly preparing itself. Like a farmer's field torn open by the plow blade in great, blood-dark ribbons, I lie fallow and silent, vacant and waiting. I've planted nothing. I want the plow gashes to remain raw and empty. And yet I can feel the stir of something new, a new strength in my hands, a deeper breath in my lungs.

In the period since his death, any such renewal of life has seemed intolerable. How could I accept the germination in me of some new sprouting of life? But I can feel it press within me, like the tender green tendrils that poke up through the sodden ground with the passing of winter.

And suddenly it comes back to me—the turtle's head, poking out from under the lid of its protective shell. The shell is the dark, silent oblivion of death, to which we retire nightly in the forgetfulness of sleep. The day-lit world outside that shell is an unthinkable mixture of truly marvelous, beautiful, and precious things, punctuated by pinching discomforts, and at times by monstrous agonies. Anyone who is alert to the reality of this world must at times wish to be delivered of it all, to return to that sanctuary of darkness, to be enfolded again in that exquisite refuge of safety and silence. And yet, like that turtle of my childhood whose head rose up after the impact of the bullet I fired into it, some unknowable force persistently rises in us, unfazed by even the most atrocious adversity. And again the head reaches out, nosing into the unknown, sniffing at the world outside itself with an irrepressible impulse once more to live.

# 20

We almost need another word for it. There is always something shocking and uncanny about death, even when it claims a person we've never met. But when it steals someone really close to us, someone we love so much that we might rather have died in their place, the agony of death cries out for a word of its own.

In the aftermath of Oliver's killing himself, I watched with dread how close it came to killing Elaine. She remained alarmingly tempted by suicide for at least a year after his, an index of how profoundly she loved him and how utterly bereft she felt in losing him. Her family convinced her to move back to Maine, hoping that might help her, though it didn't spare her much. She continued to suffer for many years under a crushing weight of grief.

The biggest comfort came when we finally found a place in an old and tiny burial plot—Maple Grove Cemetery—and arranged to bury Oliver's ashes beneath a noble boulder, graced with a simple bronze plaque. It was deeply gratifying to both of us that it lies just a mile or two down the road from the lake at Turner. On July 24, the day after what would have been Oliver's twenty-seventh birthday, we gathered the family for a small and very moving memorial service. Maybe it wasn't an accident that, several years later, after a long period of loneliness, Elaine managed to find a welcome measure of happiness with a new man in her life.

I worried a good deal about Anna's course of recovery, but unnecessarily, as things turned out. Steeling herself to be strong for Jackson, it was as if she simply regarded being crippled by grief as a luxury she couldn't afford. In the first couple of years after losing Oliver, Anna managed to finish her graduate training and took a job as a school counselor. Three years after that, she met and married a colleague of her brother's in the Baltimore Fire Department. They eventually moved north from Baltimore to Manchester, on the border with Pennsylvania, and had a baby boy together, a twinkle-eyed little guy for whom Jack was happy to play the generous and loving older brother.

As if magically true to Oliver's prediction for him, Jack has grown up amazingly gifted in both body and mind, and blessed with a remarkable personal warmth and spark. My times with him never cease to elicit a blissful sense of déjà vu for my halcyon days with his father.

Surely the most wonderful of my experiences with Jack was during the summer after he turned twelve. Anna had finally decided it was safe to tell him what had really happened when he was just three and a half, that his father hadn't died of a heart problem but had taken his own life in despair over a drug addiction. Our agreement was that, a week after his learning the true story, Jack and I would take off together for a ten-day trip to Maine and New Hampshire.

We spent most of our time in Maine. We visited Elaine—now "Grandma Mimi"—and savored a couple of days wandering as a trio in the woods and along the rock-studded coastline of Casco Bay where Elaine and I had grown up. An afternoon's circumnavigation of Baxter Island was particularly magical. Jack and I also enjoyed a wonderful stretch of days, just the two of us, camping on the Picnic Grounds at Turner where Oliver and I spent so many happy times. The plan then included a side trip to ride the Cog Railway to the summit of Mt. Washington for an overnight stay at the Lake of the Clouds hut.

Emerging from the hut into the shivering chill of the following morning, we began our descent from the mountain but stopped just above the tree line, the panorama of the surrounding peaks still breathtakingly spread before us. At a spot just off the trail, we scattered a portion of his father's ashes that I had saved for that very purpose. It's hard to know which of the two of us was more deeply touched by the moment. The best thing, of course, was sharing it together.

In the six years since that trip, Jack has only continued to blossom. Unlike his father's crushing decline during his high school years, Jack seems to have thrived with every challenge, in the classroom as much as on the lacrosse and football fields; he was a straight-A student and a star running back. As he readied to graduate from high school, he got word that he had been accepted at a prestigious college with a nearly full scholarship. At eighteen, he remembered when, at eight years old, he gave an extemporaneous eulogy of his dad in front the big boulder at Maple Grove. He wrote his college admissions essay about the courage it took to stand up and make that speech.

For me, even now, fifteen years after Oliver's death, some core of grief remains astonishingly fresh. It can still ambush me in brief, choking spasms—in response to a movie scene, a line of poetry, a few special measures of music, a sunset, a birdsong. I'm still prone to bleed without warning.

In retrospect, I regret not joining a grief group sometime soon after losing him. It probably would have been quite helpful. I suspect that my choice of going into analysis, of indulging such an intensely private labor of mourning, was motivated in part by a vague distrust of groups and a reluctance to expose myself to others. I told myself that a group would be a waste of time. (Which was absurd, of course. Analysis was a much bigger investment of time as well as money.) It now seems like an expression of my go-it-alone impulse, the same stubborn, independent streak that drove me to my perch in the hemlock tree, gazing back at my family's home with lonely satisfaction. It was in its own way a sin of pride, as if hearing others talk about their loss might diminish the secret heroism with which I wrestled with my own desolation. Then, too, I think I wanted to linger in the excruciating intimacy of my own relationship with Oliver. I think I feared that sharing my feelings in a group would somehow compromise that precious solidarity.

And yet, what they say is true. Time heals, even against our own private will to suffer. And my time in analysis was undeniably helpful, giving me a far deeper knowledge of myself than I ever thought possible and liberating me from some of the more self-inflicted tangles of pain. But something else has happened. Something that has taken me by surprise. The analysis helped open the space for it, though I suspect that it was also a late-ripening fruit of my experience with psilocybin.

Oliver's death has left me somehow larger, more soulful, with a greater capacity for love and for savoring life. The pain isn't gone. I don't think it ever will be. But it feels like grief has hollowed me out, increasing my capacity to be open to my own feelings and those of others, as when a musical instrument is made by carving out the insides of a gourd. It is the inner void that enables the resonance. For that unlikely sense of enrichment I feel grateful to him, as if the atrocity of his death eventually delivered an unexpected gift.

It was a gift I almost refused to accept. The first step was granting myself some release from guilt. Strangely enough, it was less a matter of letting myself off the hook than of letting him go. Clinging to my sense of guilt was a means of clinging to him. Feeling guilty was less painful than the brute agony of having lost him. In the short term, his absence felt even more terrible. Then it slowly came to me. He isn't really absent. Of course, he is physically gone. But there is an important sense in which his body is the only thing missing. The rest of him, the real essence of him, never left me. There have been times over the past years when I have felt him to be more present, more connected, and emotionally closer to me than ever.

It's not a religious thing. It has nothing to do with faith in some otherworldly mansions of the dead. The basic point is much simpler. There unquestionably *is* such a thing as life after death, at least in the sense that the loved ones we lose to death never really go away. On the contrary, they're always right beside us. Even *inside* us.

It actually took some adjustment, as if I had to grant myself permission to really be with him. Now, I sometimes hear his voice echo in my own. I see things through his eyes. At times I have the sense that he sees through mine. I'm almost daily reminded of his love of clouds and find myself staring, gape-mouthed, at their wispy grandeur. I often can't resist bending over for an especially shapely little stone or a colorful leaf, exactly as he would have. Even some portion of his admirable openness to strangers seems to have enduringly woven itself into my character. His bodily absence, which initially felt like the most atrocious loss, has slowly, impossibly but undeniably, opened toward a sublime presence. The strangest thing is that what I now experience of him seems to emerge from the void of absence itself, a glow of light and warmth from out of darkness.

Part of it was the way that death winnowed my memories, separating everything accidental and situational from some essential kernel of his being. The terrible struggle of the last years of his life slowly drifted away, leaving behind everything that I most loved and respected about him. His lively blue eyes and good-humored nods come back to me anew. I can see his loose-limbed gait. I savor his love of stories and his full-on hugs. I sometimes hear his chuckle as if he were sitting beside me. Above all, I am reanimated by his magically open-eyed, open-hearted enthusiasm for adventures. But my recovered access to him was also enabled by something even more unexpected. It had to do with giving up my stubborn, tormenting demand to know.

It's hard to overstate the force of that demand. It energized my frenzied scavenging through his belongings in the immediate aftermath of his death. It kept me motivated through more than three years on a psychoanalyst's couch. It drove me, just two years after his suicide, to write the first draft of this memoir. The manner of his death made it all much worse. Knowing that a loved one ended their own life, that it was their own choice that took them from us, leaves us aching to understand the reason. And also, of course, to know what we might have done differently to prevent it. Suicide assaults us with a whole series of excruciatingly unanswerable questions.

My obsession with the unknowns of Oliver's death began to relax when I allowed myself to admit how many things I never knew about him even when he was alive. I have no idea why he was so moved by the beauty of clouds. I don't know what drew him to those little stones and odd twists of driftwood. What attached him so passionately to his beloved Anna? What rose up in him so fiercely to protect his unborn son? I can guess, but without any certainties. Or what was behind those favorite doodles of his, swooping arabesques with a suggestion of three-dimensionality? Especially toward the end, he drew them incessantly, as if practicing a kind of signature. I've sometimes wondered whether they were inspired by the pirate treasure maps we drew together in his childhood. I would add vertical lines to the contour of islands to call up the excitement of cliffs and bluffs. Did he somehow have those islands in mind? I don't know.

Over time, the unknowns about his addiction and his death have washed into the little sea of other unknowns about the unique person he was. The surprise was that it didn't feel painful. On the contrary, coming to accept what I couldn't know—about the tragedy of his death but also about him, the complicated person he was—helped bring him back to me.

The more I think about it, the more I'm struck by the basic idea. Knowing is in some important part about control. It's less about being in the moment than it is about predicting the future. Love, on the contrary, is a creature of the present. Love can fuss and fidget about the future, but mostly out of fear. What love most desires is to revel in the deliciousness of Now. In that ecstatic present, love never wholly knows. It knows *enough*, and needs no more.

What if the demand to know is ultimately an impossible, even unadvisable standard for our relations with our loved ones? At some level, all of our fellow human beings are walking mysteries. And that applies not just to strangers, but also to the ones we're closest to. We inevitably try to plumb their most intimate thoughts and feelings, but none of it is ever fully transparent to us.

Their innermost, personal reality always and intrinsically escapes us. And—this is the strangest thing of all—whether we realize it or not, that shadow of our own unknowing is part of the reason we love them as we do.

The idea violates some of our fondest notions about love. Lovers flushed with the first heart-thumping thrills of romance quite typically feel bowled over above all by the feeling of *knowing* one another, so much so that they may indulge the fantasy of having been bonded in some other time, some other life. It seems profoundly appropriate that the biblical metaphor for making love is "knowing" another, having "carnal knowledge." Such assumptions of knowing would seem to be especially unassailable with respect to the love of one's own child.

And yet, on reflection, it's possible to suspect that love's self-certainties are a cover, even a kind of defense, against a deeper engagement with something we never really understand. Think of it: doesn't the magic of a new relationship arise in no small part precisely from what we don't yet know, from the encounter with another person as an enticing mystery? And when it comes to a parent's love for their child, the assumption of seamless knowing becomes especially suspect. In our relation to our children, what often dominates has less to do with who and what they really are, in and for themselves, than with our own hopes and fears for them, concerns that are usually drawn from our own life experience, our own example.

Of course, there are many things we *do* know about the people we love—their likes and dislikes, their familiar quirks and habits, what they've told us about the highs and lows of their life so far, their predictable range of moods. But all such things are anchored in strata of history, character, and personality that we never fully fathom. And remaining mindful of those unknown depths of the others we love grounds our appreciation of the gifts their very being bestows upon us. Bowing to such unknowns is a matter of truly making room for *them*, for the irreplaceable one-off they really are.

I think of Elaine. It was a high school romance. We met when we were fifteen. Allowing for our college years mostly apart, we spent thirty years together, twenty-two of them married. It's been only in retrospect, only long after we parted, that I've become properly mindful of how much I didn't know of her. I think again of Oliver's strange confession that his descent into heroin addiction had something to do with realizing her worst fears. I, too, knew that at some level Elaine struggled with obscure fears. But I couldn't tell you what they were. I suspect that she herself didn't know. And I cannot but wonder whether, if I could have better tolerated what I didn't understand in her, the path of our relationship might have taken another course.

More than any other human experience, death rubs our noses in the limits of our knowledge. Death poses the larger question of the meaning of life altogether, of course, but it also often forces us to rethink our relations to those we've loved and lost. It is as if death tears away some tissue of assumed familiarity with the departed that concealed all manner of things for which we had no explanation—indeed, about which it never even occurred to us to construct one. It takes only a bit of honesty to admit that one of the prime functions of most funeral eulogies is to fill in that abyssal blank with warm and reassuring remembrances.

When I think of other deaths I've lived through, my maternal grandmother, Miriam, comes powerfully to mind. She was a shy and retiring person but also intensely alert and deep-feeling. She gave up a career teaching art at a small college in Ohio to return home to Massachusetts to nurse her ailing mother, then met a fellow at church, married, and gave birth to a couple of daughters. (She also, I learned from my mother after Miriam's death, was twice hospitalized for severe depression and underwent electroshock therapy.) I spent a good deal of time in her quiet company. She read to me as a child and later tenderly encouraged my early efforts at drawing. I was very deeply touched by her. And yet I cannot think of her now without experiencing a kind of vertigo. I have only the faintest idea about who she really was.

Miriam's painting of the blue-green vase crowned by a gaggle of narcissus blooms hangs downstairs beside Becky's piano. What might that image have meant to her? What was it that drew her so powerfully to drawing and painting in the first place? And why did she so completely abandon her vocation in art after she was married? I have no idea. I still have a shoebox full of souvenir postcards from the summer of 1912 when she traveled in Europe after graduating from college. Visiting with her when I was fourteen, she gave me a private tour of that very box of postcard memories, then spoke of how she carried on a correspondence for years afterward with a Dutch man she had met. I was deeply moved by that afternoon's chat, somehow all the more so because I had no idea what she was really talking about.

The most unlikely and heartrending example is my mother. Four years after Oliver's death, she finally succumbed in her long battle with Alzheimer's disease. I had loved her all my life with a quiet, sure, and profound affection. She was, without any doubt, the most selfless, unstintingly giving, and loving person I have ever known. And yet—there is something mildly traumatizing about it—over the years since her death I've slowly come to realize how much of her was always a mystery. Her own deeper joys and sorrows, her own dreams and fears, were mostly concealed from others behind the happy wrapper of her supremely unselfish and overgenerous nature. I wonder how much she concealed them from herself.

As I write this, I'm looking at a black-and-white photograph of my mother, taken by my father when I was a toddler. She's sitting beside the fireplace—yes, at Turner. She smiles out at me with those sparkling eyes that are more recognizable to me than anything in the world, yet that very gaze now seems tinged by something inscrutable. It is both painful and strangely exhilarating to realize how little I really knew her. I can almost believe that I've momentarily locked glances with a woman I've never met. And yet I love and appreciate her now even more deeply than when she was alive.

Even when we become aware of the emotional gifts we receive from those who lavish their love upon us—an awareness, I submit, that is more the exception than the rule—we rarely if ever pause to acknowledge how much the real sources and meaning of those gifts remain unknown to us. Yet the truth is that what we don't know of our loved ones, far from diminishing our relationship with them, is an enduring part of the richness of the bond that ties us to them. The really crucial dimensions of our existence, the situations that invite us to respond most authentically to life—in beauty, in love, in flights of feeling—remain in large part beyond knowing. Keats had it right: "Beauty is truth, truth beauty,—that is all / Ye know on earth, and all ye need to know."

The point at stake is better appreciated by Eastern philosophers than by most in the West. Keats's words come close to the teachings of Zen Buddhism, for example, according to which the highest attainment of wisdom is the capacity for something more than knowing—what the Zen masters call "knowing of nonknowing," *muchi no chi* in Japanese. The paradox is that it is only by accepting something of the humbling experience of "knowing nonknowing" that we most fully come to ourselves, and to life. In giving to me a harrowing life lesson about such unknowing, Oliver's death expanded and deepened my capacity for life more radically than anything had before—almost enough to tempt me with a feeling of guilt all over again.

I entered psychoanalysis in order to understand something about my relation to my son, but he ended up teaching me about psychoanalysis. Of course, there is a sense in which analysis is crucially about coming to know something unexpected about oneself. It's a process that enables us to learn something elemental about our own life, to recognize and come to terms with our neurotic self-distortions. As Freud put it, something unconscious has to become conscious. That moment of coming-to-know is indispensable. For me it was penetrating the veneer of my sunny-boy persona to become aware of my own capacity for profound sadness, and also for rage, for competition, even for violence.

But such transformative self-realizations don't culminate in any perfect transparency. Far from it. I now realize that the deepest lesson we have to learn from what Freud called his "talking cure"— that long, tough, soul-labor of lying hour after hour and saying whatever comes to mind, we know not from where nor why—is that our most intimate bonds with others crucially touch upon things we do not and cannot know, both in them and in ourselves. Learning to make allowance for that dimension of unknowing, tolerating it, even honoring and appreciating it, enables us to be enlarged and reanimated by it.

In his life, and then again in his death, my son opened me toward those core mysteries of life. In losing him, something ineffable but invaluable finally forced itself upon me, making me more deeply sympathetic with others, more liable to be touched by beauty, more sensitive to the dimension of transcendence in everything—in others, in nature, and in myself.

## AUTHOR'S NOTE

I wrote this book energized by a passion for the truth, both as a reckoning with tragedy and as a personal exploration. I omitted a good deal, to protect some people's privacy and to spare the reader too long or too exhausting an account. I was also forced—massively and somewhat artificially— to condense hundreds of hours on a psychoanalyst's couch into what seems here to be a mere handful of sessions. But all the basic contents of these pages— my memories of Oliver, of my own childhood and dreams, and of my adventures with psychoanalysis and psilocybin—are rendered in accord with an unrelenting demand for accuracy. Remaining faithful to the true details felt, if nothing else, like something I owed to my son. Something I can give back to him.

## ACKNOWLEDGMENTS

The first version of this text was written in a
frenzy during the summer months of 2008. It
was then a labor of bare survival. Since then I've
rewritten it an embarrassing number of times,
not entirely sure whether I was writing for myself
or for others, but benefiting from the advice and
support of members of my family, including my
ex-wife Elaine and my sister Barbara, both of
whom read more than one draft of the text. I also
had deeply useful and encouraging conversations
with a circle of old personal friends, including

Deb Azrael, Jean Callahan, Catriona Hanley, and Jack Huston.

My efforts were further enriched by a circle of close friends and colleagues at Loyola University. Michael Franz and Paul Lukacs saw my struggles at close range and helped me think through key parts of the book. Matt Mulcahy commented on his own and also connected me very usefully with his sister, Patricia Mulcahy, a professional editor who provided very useful feedback. Mark Osteen, who has penned an exquisite memoir of his own dealing with his son's autism, *One of Us: A Family's Life with Autism*, read the manuscript and gave me valuable advice.

I'm especially grateful to my friend of half a century and colleague in the Philosophy Department, Drew Leder, who thought up the title for my very first book and also suggested the title for this one. Tim Stapleton, dear friend, mentor in teaching philosophy, and punisher on the pool table, combed over the penultimate draft with meticulous care and offered dozens of spot-on suggestions. Strike that adjective!

The book also benefited from conversations with good friends in the larger academic world, including Adrian Johnston and his wife Kathryn,

and also Todd McGowan, with whom I've
extensively and very gratefully discussed not just
this book but virtually everything I've thought
about and written for more than a decade.
Todd is a friend who feels like a brother. I'm
also grateful for valuable feedback from my
friend Benjamin Hall, a physician with extensive
experience with addicts and addiction.

Both the book and its writer have hugely
benefited from collaboration with Judith Gurewich.
It was Judith who many years ago introduced me
to Bonnie Nadzam, author of the novel *Lamb,* who
crucially helped me in beginning the transition
of this work from a tortured personal journal to
something resembling a book that other readers
might be able to tolerate. The book was later
transformed by Judith's signature method of
coaching writers, that of hosting an intimately
focused reading of the entire text in a series of
two-hour face-to-face sessions. Her input was
invaluable in giving the book its final shape.

Working with Judith on this project was
all the more meaningful for me as we had
been graduate students together in Cambridge
and Boston in the mid-eighties. We were both
finding our way into the dauntingly subtle and

demanding psychoanalytic theory of Jacques Lacan, and we read a whole shelf of Lacan's untranslated seminars together, line by line, over a span of years. Her help with this book felt like a second dispensation of the miraculous.

My last and deepest expression of gratitude goes to my wonderful partner, Rebecca Nichols. She saw me through every hour of my fifteen-year struggle to survive my son's death with unstinting patience, sensitivity, generosity of spirit, and constancy of love. On top of all that, she also read and commented very perceptively on a whole series of drafts of this book. Virtuoso violinist that she is, she also has a great eye for writing. Our shared tears and smiles have been my salvation.

RICHARD BOOTHBY is Professor of Philosophy at Loyola University Maryland. He is the author of the forthcoming *Embracing the Void: Rethinking the Origin of the Sacred,* as well as *Sex on the Couch: What Freud Still Has to Teach Us About Sex and Gender, Freud as Philosopher: Metapsychology after Lacan,* and *Death and Desire: Psychoanalytic Theory in Lacan's Return to Freud.*